A Sistermony

Books by Richard Stern

Golk

Europe or Up and Down with Baggish and Schreiber

In Any Case (reprinted as *The Chaleur Network*)

Teeth, Dying and Other Matters

Stitch

Honey and Wax

1968. A Short Novel; An Urban Idyll; Five Stories and Two Trade Notes

The Books in Fred Hampton's Apartment

Other Men's Daughters

Natural Shocks

Packages

The Invention of the Real

The Position of the Body

A Father's Words

Noble Rot. Stories 1949–1988

Shares and Other Fictions

One Person and Another

A Sistermony

A Sistermony

by Richard Stern

DONALD I. FINE, INC.

New York

Library of Congress Catalogue Card Number: 94-68096

ISBN: 1-55611-427-3

Manufactured in the United States of America

10   9   8   7   6   5   4   3   2   1

Designed by Irving Perkins Associates

Portrait of Ruth Elinor Stern, 1934 by Gilbert Sackerman.
(Photograph by Ralph Leviton)

Prologue

$\mathcal{A}$t seven A.M. on August 21, 1991, my brother-in-law, Ralph Leviton, called me in Chicago to say that his wife, my sister Ruth, had died half an hour ago. His always businesslike voice—a self-enforced monotone—wavered. "I'm sorry, Richard."

The night before, he'd called to say that the doctor had just told him that Ruth would die in the next forty-eight hours. I bought a plane ticket for a morning flight.

I thought I'd habituated myself to the idea of Ruth's death; to a degree, I had, but now I felt what I'd never felt for her before, an almost despairing love. This was mixed with relief that the contracted, grotesque, agonizing life of her last days was over and relief that the pain, tension, sadness, and discomfort of attending on it was over as well. My head was hot, my heartbeat conspicuous. I was conscious of an excited pitch of knowledge that something crucial had happened, something even larger than the very large fact that my only sister no longer existed. I said—out loud—"Ruth is dead. My poor little girl is dead." Sixty-seven, four years older than I, and, for the first time in my life, I was calling her "My poor little girl."

For a time, Ruth and I had not been close. Or so I thought. So I felt. We were so different, and the ways we were alike I despised—in my self, and in her: fear-ridden overcaution, an anal drive for orderliness, penny-pinching (countered by bursts of generosity in me, a small, steady, willed charitableness in her).

Together any length of time, we argued. When I was young, she felt I was pesty; grown, she thought me arrogantly insensitive to her and her feelings. I felt she was stupid, willfully, woefully ignorant and resentful. She bored me. I didn't like that she thought me more intelligent than I am, though her thought was often just the setting of some dumbness of mine that undercut what our father sometimes called my "highfalutin ideas" (few of which I bothered to talk about with him or her). I thought Ruth too readily accepted my indictments; they became her own, and she thought herself worse, weaker, stupider, clumsier than she was. This is how she protected what self-respect she had. Comedy was another protection, healthier because it was directed at and shared by others, including me. We were never so close as when we laughed.

In the last twenty years, though, Ruth and I discovered that we were the only people who could talk to each other about much that mattered more and more to us. We were each other's only witness, only corroborator, only judge, only companion to a million unimportant things that turned out to be important. Coincidentally—coincidentally? I'm not sure—I began to notice beautiful streaks in what had so long seemed to me her narrow, harsh, undeveloped nature. The first—revealed by egotism—was her loyalty to me and my work. For years, I'd felt oppressed by her resentment of me. I understood it, even pitied its source, but it did not bring us closer. When I realized her loyalty and devotion—in remarks quoted to me by her friends—I was surprised, moved, thrilled. Where had I been? How could I have failed to see her support? Even if it existed to protect herself, or to convert resentment into decoration, it felt good to me. Ruth was not just another friend or fan but one who would stick much longer and go much further. It didn't matter that the devotion could be analyzed in terms of self-interest. It existed, it felt wonderful to me, even as I discounted its objectivity. My mind took the shortcut—is it that?—and called it "love."

Sisterly love. (Why isn't there an English word for it?) Whatever tangle of feelings it stood for, I had it. It was at least as fundamental as resentment.

It showed itself most when I was in trouble (during illness or my divorce). Once again I became the little brother she'd walked to school, shown off, protected (and bullied). I sometimes enjoyed this

Ruth E. Stern,
circa 1950–51

role, and played to it, exaggerating my trouble. When devotion over-reached itself, and became proprietary, I took off; but, on the whole, our long undeclared war was over.

Years earlier, my version of brotherly love sprang from pity at seeing Ruth hurt. I hated that, and hated those who hurt her. I saw her snubbed and saw her lonely. Many evenings I'd take off, leaving her home alone, reading and listening to the radio. (A very few times I changed plans and stayed with her, or at least read in my room.) "Have a good time, Rich," she'd call. I'd think something like, "Oh God, Ruth, why not you, too?" I couldn't show what I felt; it would spell out the humiliation. I'd take the elevator down and walk along Central Park West thinking how much better, funnier, more decent she was than most of the girls people like me were taking out.

Partly to save money, partly from inertia, partly from fear of being alone, Ruth lived at home with our parents till she was thirty. She fell in love several times, and sometimes men fell for her, but I never knew or much cared how far things went. I was away, and heard only bits of what went on, usually when they were over. I do remember her being hurt by one fellow, a reporter. He'd "led her on," then "dumped her." I saw him once, a big meaty guy with a nasty grin. Ruth told me some of the lies he'd told her. (I don't remember them.)

In her mid-thirties, she met Ralph and, in a couple of years, married him; she loved him till the end. Age thirty-nine, she had their son, Roger. For years, too few of her sentences didn't include "my husband" or "my son." Their existence, the logo of her fulfillment, reversed thousands of bad hours.

She did have other sources of self-esteem. She was a good friend to many; she'd been a scrupulous and reliable employee of Western Electric, then Simon and Schuster, where she became Personnel Manager and Supervisor of Contracts. She loved being around authors and editors. That I became a published author advanced this

Ruth and Ralph, with Kate Stern holding Roger, 1966

sense of belonging to what counted. On letters she sent out from Simon and Schuster, she rubber-stamped the titles of my books. (Until my slighting review of their blockbuster-to-be, *Catch-22,* appeared in the New York *Times Book Review,* I was *persona grata* there.)

Ruth was also a self-consciously conscientious good citizen. She reported official and other malfeasance to authorities; wrote, circulated, and signed petitions; Election Days, she worked at polling places; Thanksgivings, she and Ralph served dinner at settlement houses. Ten days before her death, she telephoned the *Times* to protest the new glossy stock on which they printed the Sunday *Magazine.* "You can't use a ballpoint pen on the crossword puzzle." The dear *Times* thanked her, said there'd been only one other complaint, and mailed her the puzzle printed on standard stock.

Ruth told people, "I never wanted to do or be anything. I'm too lazy."

If she believed this, I didn't. It was just that ambition, like much else in her, was knotted with tics, fears. Uneasy, she flew around tidying, bossing, yelling. Warm, sweet and merry when she was sure of herself, she was exceptionally gauche and phony when she wasn't. She became a version of the mother she criticized for the faults they shared: nagging, fussiness. Their nagging was driven by suppressed resentment and, beneath that, profound anxiety: nagging released the energy of their powerless resentment. Mother's mania for cleanliness became a joke she converted into tribute to her hatred of dirt and love of order. Ruth, too, was a loud, neurotic champion of order. Unlike Mother, though, she preferred action to setting. For both, the dinner table had to be *just right, spotless* (glasses, silverware, dishes, napkins). As to food, they differed. For Mother, it was something to be finished as soon as possible; the dining room had to be restored to readiness for the next bout of disorder. Then too, Mother was proud that she didn't—and didn't have to—cook. Ruth was a fair cook who thought she was a good one; she enjoyed cooking, eating, and conversation set to the music of knives, forks, and grunts of pleasure. After her little dining nook emptied, though, she eliminated the debris of consumption as fiercely as Mother did.

Like Ruth, I was raised in Mother's cult of the immaculate, and

Richard, Mother, Ruth, November 11, 1978

despite rebellious outbreaks of sloppiness, breakage, filth, and obscenity, it has controlled my nature, perhaps even my prose.

Ruth's outbreak was intake: the tics which knotted her youthful grace. She looked like someone who didn't care what other people thought of her; sad insouciance, it was the beginning of the self-protective retreat which later called itself "lack of ambition." She was not this way with her close friends, Adele Kraus, Wilda Slevin or our cousin, Doris Lewin. With them, and sometimes with me, she was at ease, which meant a great deal of laughter—often, I thought, listening to it, sourceless and pointless, although I preferred it to her mother-mimicking pickiness and nagging.

After the death of our parents in the late 1970s, we grew much closer. Meeting and leaving, we hugged and kissed. Ruth occasionally called me "dear." I was less at ease with endearments. Contrary to the fairly recent notion that men should express feelings with ease —cry when we feel like crying, hug when we feel like hugging—I respect impassivity: one has feelings, one keeps them to oneself. (In this way, they're enriched.) Occasionally, though, I find myself letting go, sometimes unexpectedly, involuntarily. I've not only not minded that, I've congratulated myself on my emotional wealth and

Marion Veit Stern (Mother) and Henry George Stern (Daddy), 1978

generosity; but until the last years of her life, my sister and I were as economical with endearments as we were with money. Ruth had never in her life called me "darling," and we'd certainly never said that we loved each other. No one in our family would say anything like that, even to a spouse or small child. Although we grew up in an affectionate, loving family, that was our style. I did kiss my father's cheek, as I did my mother's, until the last day I saw him, but that was the only slightly unusual display of affection. We never did what, say, my wife's family does (and what I do pleasurably with her sisters), kiss on the mouth. I never hugged or was hugged—as an adult—by my father, nor, I believe, was he by his. This expression of masculine affection came to the United States during World War II and, I think, had to do with its emotional farewells and reunions. In our family, the ethnic source of reserve was the German-Jewish admiration for England and English manners. For all I know—I'm no student of the subject—the German kings of England could be the source of "English reserve"; or perhaps it goes back to the English school's Latin curriculum with its celebration of Roman stoicism. (Yet Erasmus, in the early sixteenth century, was delighted by English affection—the kisses for visiting strangers—and today many enjoy the endearments lavished upon customers by English shopkeepers.) Perhaps English-

German-Roman reserve can be traced to the layers of cloth and skins with which bewintered northerners shield themselves from cold. Hugging such bundles isn't all that satisfying.

Die, dying, death.

These old Teutonic words have always meant what they mean now. We learn them young, and know they're serious, although it usually takes decades to feel their force. When my grandchildren, aged six and three, were told that "Aunt Ruth was dying," they could not stop asking about it. Shortly after I came up from seeing Ruth in the New York hospital to see them in Weekapaug, Rhode Island, six-year-old Liza asked me, "Is Aunt Ruth really going to die?"

"Yes," I said.

"Are you angry about it?"

"Not angry. Sad."

Three-year-old Alex put in the word that was most common in his vocabulary: "Why?" ("Why is Aunt Ruth going to die?")

"Everyone dies sometime," I said. "Aunt Ruth has lived a long time." (This I didn't believe: she was twenty-four years younger than my father at his death.) "It's part of life, the way morning, afternoon, and night are different parts of the day."

Liza, a stickler, said, *"Night* isn't *day."*

"Right, but in any case, you don't get angry at night, do you? It's just different from afternoon and morning."

" 'Cause you go to bed."

"Right. You go to sleep."

I was glad she didn't ask about a "next morning" for Aunt Ruth.

Death and dying stand for totally different states. There are many sorts of dying. I remember reading *The Magic Mountain* in 1947 (after mind-killing work in the Bon Marché department store in Evansville, Indiana) and being struck by the remark of Hofrat Behrens that we start dying the moment we start breathing, since breathing is a form of oxidation, of rusting. This was the ingenious palliation of Mann's garrulous physician. The dying I mean has to do with those days before our last day, unless that last day is caused by an accident from without or within our system. Dying means our body is breaking down; we're less and less mobile; we usually feel rotten. We are, though, alive, and being alive implies expecting to live at least somewhat longer. Very few dying people anticipate the moment of their death. (Those who are going to kill themselves or die before a firing squad have very different problems, most having to do with the fact that their bodies are often in pretty good shape.) Days before her death, that is, when I saw her last, Ruth still wanted to *be*. Perhaps another way of saying this is that she was still *herself*. Dying can be an intense, even beautiful form of life, though the die-er (a useful neologism) is seldom beautiful. Imagery for the—rare?—beauty of dying is drawn from autumn or the flare of embers.

About ten days before Ruth's death, the *Times* published an unusual front-page story about a book which in a few days had sold out a huge first printing. This was *Final Exit,* the suicide manual by Derek Humphry of the Hemlock Society. It gave specific, practical advice about killing oneself. A few hours after Ruth's burial, I drove to Connecticut with my old friend Howard Goodkind, a member of the Hemlock Society. As the countryside grew more beautiful with each mile west and north, we debated—and joked about—suicide. The jokes had to do with the fears of motel owners about guests signing in with copies of the book, with crematorium trucks scooping up the bodies laid out every morning on the curb and other services required by the new suicide industry.

A few hours before, at Ruth's funeral service, I'd said that Dying was a kind of sculptor who stripped away pettiness and meanness to reveal the real person at her purest, if not best. Even physically, I'd found my dying sister beautiful, though she was fleshless as a crucifix, and barely resembled the person she'd been weeks before.

An intense, thoughtful, witty man who, in his late twenties, had been editor-in-chief of a publishing house—his biggest success was the bestseller of the fifties, Grace Metalious's *Peyton Place*—Howard had become well-to-do early and retired at fifty. He and his wife, Ruth's dear friend Adele, their children grown, had moved to

Litchfield, Connecticut. Howard studied archaeology at Yale, took piano lessons, canoed on the Bantam River, was on the Litchfield planning commission, read widely and had many friends. *But*—if this is the proper conjunction—Howard was an enthusiast for ending life "when the right time comes," and was prepared, he said, to kill himself.

"How will you know the right time?"

"I'll know."

"You may lose some fine days."

"I'm willing to lose weeks, even months."

I don't know how Ruth felt about these dying weeks, know only how I feel about them. They were intense and charged with every sort of feeling, dismay, grief, sadness, rage, fear, puzzlement, affection, passion, appetite. More, they gave—as well as took from—me my sister.

After Ralph's call that morning, my wife Alane kissed me and said, "I'll be your sister now."

Alane Rollings Stern and Richard Stern

"No," I said. "You're everything, but only Ruth's my sister."

That was somehow important. Why should a relationship which had nothing to do with choice, thus reason, be so important? (If Ruth and I had been separated at birth, I don't think it would be.)

At O'Hare, I tried to concentrate on the New York *Times*' account of tanks leaving Red Square and the Russian White House. Mikhail Gorbachev and his still-terrified and partly paralyzed wife, Raisa, their daughter, son-in-law, and granddaughter were flying back to Moscow from their Crimean *dacha,* where conspirators of the Emergency Committee had kept them under house arrest. Millions of people were rethinking their lives, wondering where they stood and might stand. Some were killing themselves.

The adjustment to Ruth's death was more modest, but for me, of course, much more intense and significant. For weeks, perhaps months—since I first realized she was going to die—I'd been doing what I've done for forty years, trying to make the kind of sense of it that could become a book. After visiting her hospital bed a few weeks ago, I'd thought of a title. It was related to the one Philip Roth had used for the account of his father's last years and legacy, *Patrimony*. There was, however, no word in any language I knew for a sister's bequest. I decided to invent one: *sistermony.* Neither the *Oxford English Dictionary* nor Cassell's Latin/English one supplied a meaning for the suffix "-mony." I thought of words which contained it— *testimony, matrimony, acrimony, alimony.* They suggested a meaning something like "the act or function of" *testes* (witness), *mater* (mother), *acer* (sharp, pungent), and *alia* (other), but there was quite a gulf between *patrimony,* meaning "bequest," the "act" of a father, and *matrimony* as the act or bequest of, or better, the prefatory action of, a mother. *Testimony* was relatively clear, but *acrimony* and *alimony* weren't. I telephoned my colleague, Prof. Arthur Adkins, who told me that unlike Greek, where you can usually find a meaning for every part of a word, Latin became derailed by its sledgehammer accents, and so covered up the sources for what were now abstract suffixes.

I knew that one difference between Roth's book and mine would be that Herman Roth had always been a powerful presence in his son's life and writing. Different versions of him appeared in many

Roth books, and in the thirty-five years I'd known Philip, I'd always heard stories about his father. As Herman created Philip, so Philip had spent years creating him, fathering his father. Since *Patrimony*, Herman had become an American character, up there with Hester, Huck, Holden and Herzog. Roth's mail was thick with letters from weeping and laughing admirers of the fierce old defender of Newark, America, FDR and the Jews. The indefatigable retailer of opinions, the impassioned clutcher of the insignificant, had been made to signify, to count. I'd met him several times, and though the meetings were filtered through Philip's fictional versions of him, the core of those versions was the remarkable man himself. He was a powerful character. Ruth wasn't. Nor had she played—or so I believed—a crucial part in my life. Only once had she shown up in my fiction, and there she'd been transformed (more, even, than Herman had been in Philip's various versions). What I knew and felt about her wasn't—I thought—a tithe of what Philip knew and felt about Herman.

That had to be a point of my book. The fact that I didn't realize what she was, in herself or to me, till her last days made the planned book something like Hemingway's "The Short Happy Life of Francis Macomber," the story about a man who comes into his own in the last minutes of his life, a life ended by the wife who realizes that Macomber's last minutes had changed him so much that he'd leave her. Ruth too was leaving, but leaving the knowledge in me that until these last days I hadn't realized what she was to herself or to me. Her sistermony was her self, the special, unrealized gift of sisterness.

Grandfather, Father, Brother

For most of my life, I've lived by the academic calendar, which makes summer a very special time. With peculiar convenience, many important events in my life have happened in the summer: the births of three of my four children, the deaths of my mother and sister.

In the early years of my first marriage, while the children were growing, I spent most summers with them in northwest Connecticut at Twin Lakes, or in the house my father-in-law built in Weekapaug. After that, I traveled a bit, sometimes teaching abroad, sometimes looking at places which figured in the books I was writing. Young, a teenager, I'd been bitten by wanderlust. At twenty-one, I got a Fulbright Fellowship to teach in France. After a year there, I moved to Germany, where my oldest son was born. We came back to the United States in 1952, and I didn't go abroad for ten years, when once again thanks to the Fulbright program, the six of us spent fifteen months in Italy and England. Since then, I'd managed to see at least the tamer regions of six of the seven continents. The old desire to travel had largely spent itself. I had the unearned confidence that I could be at home any place in the world, excepting the poles, the mountains, the jungles, the deserts, the oceans—in fact, most of the silent, empty earth. Where there were people, though, where there was some sort of society, I thought I could fit in, and not only feel at relative ease but keep a sort of Zeus-like distance from what was happening around me. Travel was a shortcut to knowledge and superiority. It was also a pressure-cooker form of diversion, a way of

In Venice on the Guidecca, 1962–63:
Gay, Christopher, and Kate Stern
Richard (holding Nick) and Andrew Stern

seeing, feeling and Rolodexing, if not understanding, the great sight-works of the world. One was *free* of familiar demands, concerns, routines. In their place was the intimacy of transience, the pleasure of those capsule histories travelers exchange, the intoxication of losing oneself in other people, places and times; all this was taken in with the pleasure of exotic food and drink served up as one took in exotic events, with new intimacy. In a small way—I've never mastered any of the languages I've crudely used—I satisfied my old desire to be a man of the world.

Even this summer, Ruth's last, I'd been ready to spend a few weeks abroad. My friend, the poet, essayist and memoir-writer Michael Anania, had worked out an exchange between four American writers and four members of the still-existing Soviet Writers' Union. Michael, who like a few poets I've known, has a flair for business deals—municipal, national and international—and is, as well, a sort of cardinal of Illinois literary affairs, had arranged the exchange, but the financing had fallen through. "Not on their side, but ours." Curious as I was to see the amazing things going on in the dying USSR, something in me was glad of that. That something needed to be within easy reach of Ruth.

Still, I wasn't then thinking in terms of weeks, even of months, left in her life (though back in April, when the bank sent me a new supply of checks, I'd wondered if she'd be alive when they ran out), and several times since, I'd found myself wondering if she'd be alive "at this time next year." I usually decided that she would be, that my speculation was a form of *Schadenfreude,* a thrilling joy in the terrible. Even as I hated her sickness and feared losing her, part of me *wanted to mourn* her.

In any case, I arranged a June trip to see her in New York. There were other reasons to go there: first to see Christopher, my oldest son, whom I hadn't seen in a year and a half (seeing him was sometimes more difficult than seeing the president of the United States); then, too, I'd signed with a new publisher and wanted to meet him; finally I wanted to see friends, especially my close friend Philip Roth. First, though, I flew to Washington to see my daughter Kate, her husband Jeff Baron and their children, Liza and Alex.

* * *

Like actors in repertory companies, we play such different roles with different people that they hardly recognize us in other roles. In life, though, there's not much of a script, and the division between acting and being is blurred. Grandfatherhood was a role I was still learning. It began one summer day in 1985 when I got a telegram from Jeff about Liza's birth. That night I walked the empty streets of Hyde Park thinking that in sixty or seventy years, decades after my death, there'd be someone on the earth to whom my being had been indispensable, someone who might, now and then, think of me. I don't remember feeling this way when my own children were born. What I remember feeling then was excitement, perhaps exaltation, relief, fatigue, vanity and flashes, perhaps flashing weights, of new responsibility. There was much to do, sending messages to grandparents, worrying and caring about my wife and the new child, making sure that we had everything we needed. This second generation—wonderful word—was something else. It was removed, almost abstract, an idea of transmission, unencumbered by immediate responsibility. There was something of art, if not design, in it. There wasn't the jolt of parenthood: I didn't see the just-born Liza, her face, neck, hands, fingernails, belly, feet, the miniature compact completeness of this flesh, this person. One was inventing a relationship, imagining a granddaughter, a little human being with her own womb, which meant the possibility of even further extension of one's own elements, perhaps an extension of interest in one's work, a book great-grandfather had written, a laugh at words put down a century before by an unknown connection (now somehow known). Our mother's father, Josef Veit, who died in 1912, when she was fifteen, left behind some letters and poems in English and German, as well as seven or eight patents for inventions he'd worked on or backed. These poems and patents were special to Ruth and me, though we didn't understand the chemical processes, and the words in the letters and poems are banal. They were a handshake over time, an intimate self-extension, a flesh-and-blood prosthesis. In the birth of your own children what dominates feeling is relief that all's gone well and—in my case —pride in this assertion of manliness and potency. As you got to know the child, there was the unexpectedly passionate pleasure in having—yes, having, "owning"—something so deeply different and lovable. (I was lucky enough not to worry about being able to take care of the children, although I had nothing in the bank except what I put in each payday.)

The night of Liza's birth I also thought of relatives and friends who didn't have children, and of the problems this posed for them about their own existence and sense of completeness. I related this sense to my own feelings that my work had less success than that of such friends as Roth and Bellow. Like genetic stoppage, this constituted—in my feeling, if not my reason—a diminution of what I call, for want of a better word, *manhood.* ("Humanity" won't do here, for that's something which can't—or shouldn't—be enriched by medals, fame or an egoistic sense of self-fulfillment.) Something pretty deep in me says a man impregnates, generates, works and makes a mark. Our father, whose modesty did not diminish self-respect, would not have had such thoughts. *Manliness,* yes, that was important, but it was an adolescent concept used only after you got "your first piece." (I'm drawing here on the little memoir he wrote and Ruth edited and published.) As for Ruth, she'd have regarded such notions as the masculine crowing which allowed her and other *normal* women to go on with the real business of life, being—and looking—decent and getting through each day, season and year with minimum difficulty.

Of course, my childless friends are spared much as well, including the sense of loss I would now feel if Liza and Alex did not exist. That loss exists only after knowledge, after the special gift Kate and Jeff had given me. (Not that a gift was on their minds when they gave it.)

In Bethesda, watching Liza dressed for Flag Day in red, white and blue sing patriotic songs with her class, or seeing her and Alex at a wedding where they buzzed around like yellowjackets among the flowers, I was in another dimension of grandfatherhood, the public display of one's treasure. That treasure had to do with self-extension in time. Three generations. One had somehow "done it," though, God knows, the "doing" was little more than living, if not living it up. In any event, I wished my parents had lived long enough to enjoy this genetic layer and hoped I'd see Liza and Alex's children.

Sharper than these feelings was the hope that my sons, a decade or, in Christopher's case, two decades older than I when I became a father, would one day feel what I was feeling.

That they weren't fathers now had, I thought, something to do with me. What it was I didn't know, but it had to do with something I'd failed to do, or that I hadn't done right. Their single state was a criticism of the way I'd handled my doubled one. (The egotism of this may suggest the way.) What weakness, bad behavior, lack or deformity had they felt or seen in me which kept them from being youthful fathers? Andrew had married at about the same age I had, but it hadn't lasted. He'd been with many girls since, and he'd asked at least one to marry him, but at thirty-four, he, like his older and younger brothers, was unmarried. Chris and Nick had been living with very nice girls for years, but shortly after Nick gave his girl, Kirsten, a ring, they decided to break up. Somewhere in here I figured I figured—and not well.

My unhappiness that my sons did not enjoy this slice of my happiness was augmented by the sadness that Ruth would not have, or at least know, her grandchildren. Roger had been the largest and sweetest—if, at times, most difficult—part of her life. A grandchild would have been a tremendous joy for her.

In a house with three generations, there's much consciousness and much talk about age. Much of Liza's conversation bears on the difference in her and Alex's ages, and Kate and Jeff and their friends, just hitting forty, magnify little signals of decline, feeling them more acutely than they would in ten years, when they'd accept them as a matter of course.

To have my children and their friends becoming what they thought of as old meant that I, much older, was also—to use one of the overused words of the eighties—a survivor, a good thing to be. There's a miser's sinister pleasure in living long, and though my expectation—shadowed now by Ruth's early death—is that I'll live a good deal longer, the fact that I'm in my seventh decade gives me unreasonable joy. ("Unreasonable," for once again, I've done nothing to deserve it except have genes and be cautious to the point of cowardice.)

*   *   *

One afternoon, in charge of Liza while Kate took Alex to a birthday party, I got ready to take her out. She pointed to a tie on the table and asked if I were going to wear it.

"Yes," I said. "Unless you think it doesn't go with the shirt." (Red-green blind, I'm used to asking people to pick out ties for me; it was a special pleasure to enroll Liza.)

"It goes," she said. "You're going to look smashing."

Though I know *smashing* was scooped from Kate and Jeff's large language bins, its unexpectedness pleased me. At breakfast, I'd asked Liza why she preferred Cheerios to the bran flakes I ate. *"De gustibus non disputandum est,"* she said. This also pleased me, though it was more like a trick. Liza adores words and already knows and appreciates different language systems. (When the Barons returned to the States from two years in Japan—Jeff's a foreign service officer—she spoke to—through!—me only in Japanese.) This interest doesn't substitute for but enriches her powers of observation. In any case, the continuity of a family interest in words delighted me. So did our excursion to the park, though the delight was laced with fatigue and self-denial (denial, that is, of my *normal* range of speech and behavior, the consequence of *playing,* as well as *being,* "Grandpa"). Liza and I were a little team, bound to each other by—call it *familiarity.* If, God forbid, things happened which only the two of us survived, we would, by virtue of this familiarity, assume the responsibility of taking care of each other. Even now Liza saved me from taking the wrong path to the park. No wonder "A little child shall lead them" is scriptural. To be comforted, let alone instructed and led by one's own —partial—creation is a beautiful form of self-expansion.

When we got home, Liza called her friend Maggie to explain why she couldn't visit her. "One, my grandfather's here. Two, my mother isn't. Three, I have to have a bath. Four, I have to have supper. Five, my father's coming home. Six, I have to go to bed." This was repeated for several minutes with variations, and a remarkable gamut of facial expressions. In Liza's mixture of politeness and firmness, precision and patience, I was reminded of Ruth. Like Ruth, too, Liza was a comedian, not so much a performer as a person who loved word and body play and was delighted when other people

Grandpa Richard Stern with Kate and Liza in Fukuoka, Japan, 1987

were delighted with it. In her relationship to Alex, I saw some of Ruth's relationship to me, the possessiveness and protectiveness of the older sister, as well as annoyance, jealousy, rivalry and fury. (I think Alex is better-humored and tougher than I was.) That they're three, not four years apart, may make them a closer team.

I left for New York by train. After we dropped Liza off at school —in school mode, she politely allowed Grandpa a farewell kiss— Kate and Alex took me to Union Station.

I hadn't been there since college days, when I sometimes changed trains here. In those days of World War II and its aftermath, the station was full of servicemen sitting on duffel bags or making for trains, their wives, mothers and girlfriends trailing them. "Colored" passengers going south had to shift to segregated cars. (Memory of that outrage—which I hated, but did nothing about—should have spiked nostalgia. It didn't. Like death, nostalgia is a great revisionist.) Now it was wonderful being in the train, hearing the sepulchral announcements: "Balll-t-maur," "Willl-min-tn," "Phil-la-*delph*-i-ya." The train I took several times a year to Raleigh was called the Silver Meteor. In August 1947, having graduated from Chapel Hill, I said goodbye to the first passionate love of my life, Jo Bledsoe. She and I lay in a grassy ditch, yards from the Raleigh station tracks, minutes before her train would take her to pre-Disney Orlando and the Meteor would take me north to New York. My stomach was a rock, my eye sockets couldn't hold my eyes, I wanted to die. Forty-five years later, I remembered feeling that my body wasn't big enough to hold those feelings. There wasn't an ounce of redemptive sweetness in them, and I didn't have one ounce of nostalgia for those moments.

Now, I said goodbye a little tearfully to Kate and Alex, who in the enormous station seemed fragile and tiny. (Was this the point of these monumental buildings?) I had the New York *Times,* my notebook, two seats to myself, and I was going to meet Richard Marek, the publisher, and to see Ruth, Christopher and Philip.

Suddenly, I was sure that I *wouldn't* see Christopher. He hadn't answered the letter in which I'd given him my New York dates, and I hadn't phoned to confirm them. Now I was almost daring him not to see me, and enjoying a foretaste of the righteous anger I'd feel at this filial defection. I asked myself—in my journal—what was going on, what was wrong with me? No wonder this son of mine often wouldn't see me. I'd never opened the gates to myself. How could *he* get through?

No reeds in the world are as befouled and resistant as those in the antibiotic filth of the Jersey marshland. A relief when the Meteor goes into the tunnel under the river to Manhattan. In Penn Station, cops eyed the con artists and loafers (a favorite word of my father, which Ruth and I still used). In the ninety-degree heat of New York, I walked to Seventh Avenue and got a ride in a springless, un-air-conditioned cab with a driver named Singh, unturbanned and unbearded, so, at most, an ex-Sikh. (The line remembered from my few weeks in India is "All Sikhs are named Singh, but not all Singhs are Sikhs.") This Singh, thirtyish, thin-mustached, was a frenzied ear-picker. We drove north on Eighth Avenue, filthy, ugly, noisier than ever, the filth, noise and ugliness augmented by construction workers tearing up the west side of the avenue. No wonder Singh worked away at his ear.

The doorman at Ruth's apartment gave me the key. "Miz Leviton say to tell you she be back soon." Ruth's apartment is on the second floor, two bedrooms, two bathrooms, a living room, a dining area, a small kitchen. The Levitons had lived there twenty years. Ralph, raised in the Bronx, had always wanted to live in zip code 10021, Manhattan's "Silk Stocking" district. His father, a hard-bitten, uncommunicative immigrant taxi driver, spoke only Yiddish, which Ralph spoke till he got to the first grade. By now he spoke and looked like any Silk Stocking.

There was a note for me on the Florentine escritoire:

Dear Rich,

Back soon. Cathy Diamond called. Chris in California and she's busy.

Love, Ruth

Prophecy fulfilled. I would not be having dinner with Christopher, with or without his companion, Cathy. Fine, I'd have dinner with Ralph and Ruth. But I was disappointed, and more than that.

I stayed in Roger's old room, which for me is still a boy's room, a miniature stage set of masculinity, though now it was Ralph's office, and there were papers, indexed public relations books and a Rolodex on Roger's desk in place of the hamster cage. I took off my travelling clothes and had a bath in the too-small bathtub. The phone rang as I was putting on a sportshirt.

"Ralph?"

"No, it's Richard. Doris?" Doris Lewin Newman is the daughter of our father's youngest sister Mildred, our mother's first best friend and exact contemporary. Our grandmother, Mildred's mother, died in 1897, days after her birth. Baby Mildred had been sent south to live with our grandmother's sister. One year later, our grandfather married the forelady of his business and Mildred was brought back and told she was the forelady's daughter. Decades later she said, "Much as I loved her, I always knew she was not my real mother." Doris and her brother, Bob Lewin, believe that this early play-acting deranged Mildred's emotional system and made her incapable of loving anyone. For Ruth and me, though, she was the favorite aunt, attentive and affectionate. We were proud of pretty, black-haired, gap-toothed Mildred with her giggly charm, and only learned about her children's negative feeling a dozen years ago, when, in the aftermath of our mother's death, Doris, in a brilliant and passionate oration, vented half a century of filial rage.

"I'm calling to see how Ruthie is."

"She's at the store. She'll be right back. Why don't you come up?"

"I will. For a minute."

"How is she, Doris?"

"You'll be shocked. She's very thin."

Doris herself is very big. She'd been a beautiful girl, one of my first images of beauty. Once a year we used to stay with the Lewins in Hazleton, Pennsylvania, where Aunt Mildred's rotund husband, Uncle Irving, ran a textile mill. Uncle Irving was a great comic, Aunt Mildred sweet and generous, Doris was beautiful and kind, and Bob, eight years older, was my idol. Above all, there was Prince, the collie, particularly precious to me because Momma said it wasn't fair to keep a dog "in a New York apartment." (Like most of us, Momma concealed her aversions beneath altruism and benevolence. A dog was a subversive threat to cleanliness and order.) Bob went off to Mercersburg, Doris to Ashley Hall about the same time that Ruth went to Julia Richman, a classmate but no friend of Lauren—Betty—Bacall-Weinstein. Sometime in between, Uncle Irving was fired; the laughter stopped till he got a job in Greensboro, North Carolina (which affected my life, because when I was rejected by Harvard, Yale and Michigan, he was able to get me into the University of North Carolina at Chapel Hill).

Waiting for Doris and Ruth, I looked at photograph albums.

Doris and
Mildred Lewin

Ruth had been an adorable little girl, very straight in her white dresses, her face attentive, thoughtful and pretty under the black bangs. With the new alertness of feminist analysis in me, I spotted a deference and restraint in her that I don't, for instance, see in Liza and didn't see in Kate. Perhaps Ruth was as expressive and innocently opinionated as Liza, but looking at those beautiful black-and-white pictures from the late twenties and early thirties I didn't remember that. When I was ten or twelve and Ruth fourteen or sixteen, she'd grown, and grown awkwardly. My mother, five-foot-four, was six inches shorter, and handled Ruth's height badly. Ruth wasn't trained to be proud of it, but shrank away from it. Self-consciousness altered her expressions. The smiles in the photographs became strained, the face tenser. The proportions too were not quite as harmonious, the nose and mouth too big for the smallish face.

I didn't think Ruth pretty back then—as Doris was—and worse,

Ruth Stern (age
4½), 1928

she didn't think she was pretty. Yet going through the albums, I saw
that at eighteen and nineteen she *was* pretty, tall, with a good figure,
full, if not *zaftig,* cool and witty-looking, a sort of Jewish Katharine
Hepburn.

Now, looking out the window, I spotted her coming along with
a grocery bag. She was bent, but, from the window anyway, she
looked better than I'd anticipated. I went out to meet the elevator,
and when she stepped out and saw me, her black eyes widened with
surprise.

"Hello, sweetheart," she said. Not the usual greeting. "What are
you doing out here?"

"I saw you coming." I took the bag, and we hugged.

Her face had lines I'd never seen before; and it was gaunt. She walked slowly; she was old. In the year since I'd last seen her, she'd moved from one plateau to this penultimate one. I suppressed the shock I felt. In the apartment she asked the hospitable questions she always asked: Did I have everything? Did I want anything to eat or drink? How was the trip? How were Kate and Jeff? How was Alane? But the pace was different from a year ago, slower, labored. There were fewer fussbudgeting gestures, a quicker resort to the couch.

"You've had quite a time, Ruthens."

"Oh God, when will it end? It's one thing after another."

"You look better than I thought you would. And you're moving around, you carry your groceries."

"Barely. One block and I'm tired. Two blocks is a marathon."

"Doris called, she's coming up."

"So attentive. Everybody's been. More than I can take. Everything wears me out. Not you. I'm so glad you came."

The house-phone buzzed, and Ruth told the doorman to admit Doris, who showed up with a bottle of special apple cider and crab meat from Rosedale, the famous fish store which her husband Bob Newman—like his father before him—owns, and which has helped make him one of the minor characters of New York life, a tough fishman who treats the twenty people who work for him and the iced, silvery bodies which surround him a good deal more courteously and affectionately than he treats his Silk Stocking customers. Only my mother and father had welcomed Bob into the family. He said this again and again (the last time at Ruth's funeral). Our aunts and uncles, Florence, Hortense, Louie and Sylvia, themselves one generation off the boat, could not reconcile themselves to the marriage of the beautiful girl from Ashley Hall to the heir of Rosedale. Doris turned her back on them, and when her two boys were of age, she worked in the store, acting as cashier, taking phone orders, joshing customers, a large, spectacular presence whom I came in to hug whenever I was within blocks. Bob, too, I liked. For years I'd meant to go down with him at four in the morning to the Fulton Fish Market, where five or six days a week he went to buy fish, his pockets stuffed with cash, for which, a couple of times, he'd been clubbed and robbed, occasions unreported to the police, for he knows the code. The toughness of this big, grizzled fellow with the popped blue eyes in his white fishman's smock isn't only for display. Seventy-one years old, he still rises day after day at three and drives to the fish market.

Recently, he and Doris had had a rough spell—something to do with his taking a woman to Europe. Doris had gone off to Santa Fe where their son Alan, his wife and children—one of whom, a Down syndrome child, Doris particularly adores—live. She was about to buy a house down there, was, indeed, leaving tomorrow to close the deal.

This is what she talked about now in her boisterous, amusing way. I thought, "If only Ruth could get a transfusion of that energy." Looking at Doris's handsome bulk, listening to her expressive talk, who could have guessed she'd had a terrible cancer? Now she was back, full-blast. "I've been talking to the broker. I need sixty thousand, cash, to close on the house, he says my margin account is messed up, I'm going to have to borrow the money from Robbie." The room filled with complaints about brokers and other obstacles to the untrammelled life, then, with an immense hug and kiss for me, and an affectionate, tender farewell to Ruth, her oldest friend, she was off.

All friends and relatives have conversational touchstones, provocative things we have in common, our own soap operas. Ruth and I had our relatives. Some were more provocative than others. On some, like Bob Lewin, I was an authority, though Ruth could fill me in on things Doris had told her about him. Ruth was the chief authority on Doris, her generosity, her bitterness, her large ups and larger downs.

Christopher was a rich subject for both of us. For Ruth, he was "a character," and I could indulge that interest to amuse, shock and anger her. (As I'd tell her to go easy on Roger, she'd tell me to go easy on Chris.) For me, Christopher was not a character, though I had used elements of him in several stories and novels. I knew him, in a way, better than I knew anyone I'd ever known, and not just because he was my oldest child, whom I'd observed, cared for, loved, taught, raised, been angered and disappointed by, seen intertwine with the lives of my other children, and talked with intimately off and on for more than thirty years (when he was ten years old). I suppose I've talked with him too much; I have played and still play too large a role in his life, or at least his head, for, wisely, he doesn't see much of me. He knows my writing, at least my fiction, better than I do, and often characterizes something I've done by referring to something I've written. He talks about my work with his analyst, perhaps with others. He thinks I need analysis, that I'm not "in touch" with my feelings, that I don't know myself as analysis has helped him know himself. "You'd be a better writer if you were." I grant him that (though I'm not so sure); indeed, these days, I usually grant him every claim. When I don't, it's wartime. No one reads me more closely—or both better and worse. I've often felt like a stone about his neck. To some degree I feel I'm a weight on all the children. (Not always in a bad way.) Andy and Nick have been able to see me a bit more distantly; they usually make me into a character they can manage, yet there've been occasions—few, thank God—when out of some trifling disagreement comes a burst of furious denunciation, hard for me to understand or tolerate, though I usually manage to do both. Ruth, too, has exploded at me, two or three times, out of the—to me— unfathomable blue.

On the couch, two or three feet from her, I consciously stirred our old family *pot au feu,* the reliable nourishment of our best talk. I asked her about the life I'd lived but didn't remember. "What's your first memory of me? Do you remember Momma being pregnant?"

She said, "I used to sit on the bathtub when she was taking a bath. I noticed her getting fat." (I thought of the Bellows' cat, Moosie, who sits on the tub when Saul takes a bath. "He wants to see what one of 'these creatures' is made like.") "She explained it was you, and asked what we should call you. We decided on Richard." Our father's mother was Rose, our mother's Regina (named, in the philo-English fashion of her day, after Victoria Regina; disliking the name, she'd changed it to Rachel). So my parents named us with "R" names to honor them. Ruth married an R, and their son is Roger. "When you came back from the hospital in the nurse's arms, you were making a

Grandma
(Rachel Veit),
Mother (Marion
Veit Stern),
Richard and
Ruth Stern,
1928

fuss. She put you down and said, 'It's all right, Sonny.' I burst into
tears. I thought your name had been changed."

I don't remember when my consciousness of Ruth became specific. She was a presence, something familiar. I'm aware of her as
both companion and opposition, someone in the room with me.
(This is a memory of the years from 1928 to 1932, when we lived at
Eighty-ninth and Broadway.) I remember her across the dark space
listening to Daddy tell us stories. In 1932, when I was four and Ruth
eight, we moved to Eighty-fourth and Central Park West (a tony

address then, as it is once again), and had separate rooms. There are memories of us there sitting on the floor, playing cards, fighting, her calling out, "Richard hit me!" (Whether I had or not.) I remember walking with her down Eighty-fourth Street to Columbus and Amsterdam Avenues, then over Broadway to West End and Eighty-second, where PS 9 was and still is. (The day after her death Christopher and I walked over to see it.) I felt her positively as guide and protector. Sometimes she walked too fast; I had to hurry, my book bag hitting my legs. I had to catch up to her.

I also remember one time—perhaps there were more, but I remember only one time—I may have been seven, eight or even nine, when I crawled into her bed, and felt surprised and happy at the warmth and special softness of her body. Had she, more conscious than I, sensed something out of line and made this the last such event?

At Eighty-ninth Street and Broadway, Daddy stood between us while he told us stories. We had those stories in common. No one else alive had them. We also had our Grandpa Stern in common. We remembered him showing off his strength by lifting the laundry hamper which the once-a-week laundress brought up from the basement. We remembered that basement, which looked like the hold of an ocean liner, full of steam and the jokes of thirty or forty black laundresses doing the wash of eighty apartments in tubs, rubbing the wet clothes on corrugated metal boards. We remembered the elevator men and doormen, Al, Frank, Harry, John, Arthur. Most were New York Yankee fans (something Ruth did not share with me). Our house on Central Park West was sacred because the Yankee third baseman, Red Rolfe, lived on the third floor, and then, miracle of miracles, Joe DiMaggio moved across the street with his actress wife, Dorothy Arnold. From my window, Ruth and I watched him drying the dishes. Every afternoon the Yankees played at the Stadium, Fiskie Benjamin and I stopped our handball game to wait in front of 241 Central Park West till Joe, sleek as a seal, got out of his taxi. "Hello, boys." "How'd you do today, Joe?" "Two for four," he'd say, hurrying past us. (I didn't wonder—as I do now—why he didn't share a cab with Red.)

Ruth and I remembered the maids Momma hired and fired,

Anna Schreck What-the-Heck, and Teresa, the dark-haired Norwegian beauty who'd worked for a Dr. Gogarty in New Jersey (who turned out to be Oliver St. John Gogarty, Joyce's Buck Mulligan). Also Tina, who played casino with me and who was the first woman I saw naked. (I peeked through the keyhole of the maid's room. I didn't know about keyholes when Teresa worked for us; I did want to see her.) Ruth also remembered the maid who stayed only an hour because when Momma told me we had a new maid from Germany, I said in my never-soft voice, "I thought we didn't like Germans."

We had radio programs in common—"Mr. Keen, Tracer of Lost Persons," "Second Husband" with Helen Menken, and the Sunday night comedians, Jack Benny, Fred Allen, Edgar Bergen and Charlie McCarthy. Once or twice, we listened to Hitler's incomprehensible gutturals, and Daddy often called us, sometimes from sleep, to hear Roosevelt's Fireside Chats. We remembered our German cousin, Elsa, whom Uncle Gus rescued "from over there." Elsa became a masseuse and once a week thumped Momma's ample flanks and back. "Come back later," she or Momma would tell me as I stared.

We remembered what every room of our apartment looked and felt like, the mahogany and velvet reserve of the living room, saved for "company" except when Momma played the piano and I sat beside her on the brocade bench.

Who stole my heart away?
Who made me rue the day?

and Daddy's favorite,

They asked me how I knew
My true love was true?
I of course replied,
'Something here inside.'
Smoke gets in your eyes.

Momma played by ear, anything and everything, all terribly but like everything else in the apartment, more beautiful in the holy waters of recollection. Ruth took piano lessons for years, but the only piece she could play was "Für Elise." She was deeply unmusical, sang terribly and, early on, sang only to mock her incapacity. (I hated that worse than her voice.)

The dining room was mahogany and solemn, or maybe just serious. Eating was serious, formal. I had to wear a coat and tie. Before that, till I was eight or nine, I didn't eat with my parents but in my room with a nurse, and later with a Columbia graduate student, a severe young woman who, said Ruth, "taught you manners." When I did join that gustatory express train, the family dinner—"Eat up so Teresa can clean up," as if cleaning up, not eating, was the crucial act —I spilled water, milk, cocoa, soup, and was rebuked. I was a slob, careless, impossible. Yet Daddy told the day's stories and listened to mine while Momma, with dainty speed, emptied her plate. (Where had the food gone?) I loved the pot roasts, potato pancakes, the rye bread and rich soups—Ruth and I competed for marrow Daddy scooped from the bone—the steaks, brown Betty, ice cream—a rare treat in those days of tiny freezers—everything but liver, beets and cooked carrots.

Ruth's room up the hall, a short L stroke from our bathroom, was *terra incognita.* ("Keep *out!"*) In my room we played cards, marbles or checkers—she didn't want to learn chess—on the floor. There'd be arguments, she'd call out, "Daddy," even when she hit me first. (Years later, she told me, "I liked to see you cry.")

My room was first shared with one Nurse Mary Quinn, then a second, unrelated Mary Quinn. When each left, I went under the bed and stayed hours, raging, until Daddy talked me out. (The brown bed slats are part of memory; I can see them now.) When Grandpa stayed over, he slept there—where did the nurse go?—and I thought him an amazing sight in his ankle-length white nightgown, his filigree silver-and-leather water bottle on the table beside the bed. For breakfast, he put butter and salt on hominy (we never called it "grits") and ate it in a spiral from the circumference to the final bite in the center. He had beautiful silk-white hair, a grand white moustache and a Hungarian accent; he called Ruth "Roosie." (He never mastered "th.")

A long hall led to Momma and Daddy's room. Their beds were separated by a table (which today holds my bedside books and radio). I went into their beds without question. When, rarely, I found them in the same bed, I didn't express my puzzlement.

Ralph came in in his long walking shorts and short-sleeved shirt. His squarish, blue-eyed, snub-nosed, gentle face was drawn in fatigued concentration. He was stooped, gray, thin. After shaking hands with me, he fussed around the tiny kitchen, then with the mail on the Florentine desk. It struck me that he was turning into the Ruth who was always stirring, fussing, tidying, fixing, storing, the Ruth who reincarnated our restless, fussing mother.

"Richard'll eat with us, honey," said Ruth. Ralph knew about the message from Cathy, about Chris being in California.

"Good," he said. "I'll make supper."

"No, you won't," said Ruth. "I'll make it. Give Richard a drink."

While she cooked, I drank scotch, and Ralph talked about the complex course of her illness and treatments, the hospital stays for the thickening in her bowel after the chemotherapy, the fear that she'd have a colostomy and have to defecate in a bag around her waist, the relief that Dr. Caputo had managed to resect the colon without that humiliating emblem of private filth. "Ruth keeps after me to go out, see friends. I try, and I try to work three times a week. The guy I work for couldn't be nicer. 'Work whenever you can,' he says. Sometimes I can't. Sometimes I have to." It was clear that since retirement a year ago from Union Carbide, his real job had been taking care of Ruth. He'd been a public relations executive, a job he'd held and hated for ten years. When the Union Carbide plant in Bhopal had released a gas which choked, maimed and blinded hundreds of Indians, Ralph had been in charge of putting a good face on this public relations disaster. Every political bone in his anticorporate body ached with duplicity. He'd come close to throwing in the towel, but he persisted: he needed a few more years for a decent pension. Ruth had eased the ache and stiffened his wavering upper lip, but it was their time of troubles and in Ralph, especially, bitter dust had settled.

We moved to the "dining area" for Ruth's chicken. It was drier than usual, but I ate it in a special way, as if it were symbolic, sacramental. The meal, the last she ever cooked for me, was more a reminder than a meal. (A reminder of good meals she'd cooked over the years when I came to New York.)

The phone rang. Ralph answered. "Your father's here," he said. "Are you in California?" Then, after a minute, he looked up. "He says, 'That's complicated,' " and waved the phone at me.

I said, "I'd better take it inside." I knew Christopher's calls. Short ones lasted half an hour.

Christopher said he was not in California. "I'm on a deadline." He was ghostwriting a book for a therapist named Freudenheim, the manuscript was late, and he was afraid that if he saw me it might be such an emotional upheaval that he wouldn't be able to work for days. "I wrote you in Chicago. Didn't you get it?"

"It must have come while I was in Bethesda. I'm disappointed, but I understand. Though I was counting on seeing you."

"Next time. How are you?"

This opened the gate for an hour of talk, not one of our longer telephone talks, but long enough to bring Ruth to the door several times, lifting her eyes and shaking her head in renewed amazement at the Christopherian soap opera. I finally broke off, telling Chris that Ruth wanted to call someone. "Lots of luck with the book."

I tied up the phone a little longer calling Alane in Chicago. Sure enough, Chris's postcard had arrived. She read it to me. For the first, and, I hope, only time in his life, he'd addressed me as "Dear Richard," and signed it "CHS." (The "H" is for Holmes, a name from his mother's family.) The card said he'd be in California, and suggested some New York events I should take in. I shuttled the familiar route between exasperation and pity. (It paralleled the shuttle between guilt and love.)

Years ago, a critic, more acute than I, spotted treason as the common denominator of my first four novels. I knew that *In Any Case,* the novel explicitly about betrayal, translated specific guilt feelings. Guilt, cooked in loss, was also the dominant feeling of the fifth novel, though it could be read as a love, renewal and second-chance story. If love and lust (*Wander,* erotic and intellectual) were the manic elements of my being, guilt about harming those I love was the depressive element. Almost every paternal divorcé feels this guilt, though it may be covered by rage if he is—or feels—innocent. Of

Christopher and Richard Stern with Aunt Mildred, Bob Lewin and his daughter Lianne and son Jim Lewin, Carpenteria, California, 1968

course, it's complicated, and novels from *Anna Karenina* on express varieties of reaction to it. It took years to stop being dominated by it, but every once in a while the door opens, and through it come self-indictment and the sense of loss. It's as close as I get to something like the consciousness of sin. (Alane, who has suffered from it, has helped moderate if not eliminate it.)

Ruth went to bed early. Ralph and I talked awhile, then I went in and read one of the books Ruth had been given to read in the hospital. ("I hated it," she said.) It was Julia Phillips's *You'll Never Eat Lunch in this Town Again.* The book I'd been working on for the last few months, and to which I'll return when I finish this one, has to do with a film director in Hollywood: Julia Phillips's was up that alley. For a while, it engaged me. It's rapid, frank and full of the eighties brute writing you saw much of in *Vanity Fair* and *New York* magazine. Very few sentences lack a *cock, cunt* or *fuck,* and the deal-makers who dominate the book let almost nothing censor their expressions of hatred, egomania, need to annihilate, conquer and score. Only exhaustion, flagged and relieved by drugs, restrains them. The book is one of the ugliest I've ever read, a cinder from an almost willed inferno. No wonder Ruth hated it. The book consumes itself, for after a hundred or so pages the unremitting, unredeemed viciousness becomes as tedious as hell itself. It takes a Dante to sustain interest in more than a few circles; Julia manages half an arc. Still her book may stand with a few about Wall Street and a few other streets of mindless avarice to mark the degradation of individuality in the 1980s.

The next day, while Ruth napped, I walked down Third Avenue to see *Dark Obsession,* a pretty good movie about a madly jealous British aristocrat who connives with fellow officers to cover up a hit-and-run accident. The film is charged with class hatred, not unlike the hatred of those at whom Auden aimed his early poems, the "hunting fathers," "the hard bitch and the riding master," the "insufficient units / Dangerous, easy in furs, in uniform," "the old gang" whose annihilation the poet predicted and desired. Many did die in World War II, but here in 1991 they were again, almost as powerful as ever. The aristocrat's wife, played by Amanda Donahue, the smart, gay English lawyer on "L.A. Law" (the only TV show Ruth watched), is wonderful to look at (and one looks at all of her).

Back at Ruth's, there was a call from Philip, inviting me to join him and Paul Le Clair (the president of Hunter College) at Kalinko's on Madison Avenue, where we'd all eaten some months ago. I said I was meeting my new publisher, Richard Marek.

"Where?"

"Perigord."

"That's the right place."

Richard Marek was alone in Le Perigord, a white-haired, solid, amiable man in a blue suit and loose tie, drinking a martini. The restaurant had been his favorite for decades, he used to come for lunch when it opened. He told me his publishing history. He'd been with Macmillan, World and St. Martin's, and had been editor-in-chief at Dutton years after my editor there, Hal Scharlatt, died on a tennis court (age thirty-six). Now he was with Crown, a unit of Random House. He'd always wanted to publish a few books he loved. Delphinium had come along. "It's my jewel."

"Who owns it?"

"Two wealthy women. Carol Engel and Lori Milken. Yes, she is." (The wife of the recently jailed emperor of junk bonds.)

Marek and I had met years ago, when he was recruiting authors for Macmillan. I don't think he remembered—he politely said he did —but I did, because I used to read the music criticism of his father, George Marek. I asked about him.

"He died a few years ago. Eighty-three, working on a book about Mahler. My mother's eighty-six." He'd grown up in a musical, intellectual milieu. "My first kiss was from Sonia Horowitz."

I said I'd seen her once backstage at Carnegie Hall sitting under the piano at which her father sat exhausted after a concert, beaky head in poetic hand, while Sonia's mother, a Toscanini, shrieked at the orchestra manager to clear the room. Lots of lightning in that household. (At forty, Sonia killed herself.)

Marek said that Toscanini and Thomas Mann were his father's idols. Toscanini had come to dinner at their house; he'd never met Mann. I had and told him about it. In 1951 I was teaching illiterate soldiers in Frankfurt, Germany. My then-wife and I had tickets for the Salzburg Festival when we read that Mann was coming to Austria. Aunt Mildred had married the brother of Elias Lowe, the paleographer, whose wife was Mann's translator, Helen Lowe-Porter. I wrote for Mann's address and then wrote Mann that I was going to the festival—could I see him? He sent me directions to Bad Gastein, for *"Ihr Orientierung,"* on a small blue sheet which I displayed to the German secretaries like a piece of the true cross. In Gastein, I walked to the Manns' *pension.* There was Frau Mann, a delightful, deep-voiced woman with clipped white hair, and, in alpine hat, tweed coat and matching knickers tucked into walking socks, was the Great Man, eyes behind sunglasses. We sat on a lawn bench facing the mountains. Had I been to Gastein before? No? What had I heard in Salzburg? *Wozzek?* He said he may have met Berg, but couldn't remember. He had met Bartók. "He had the eyes of a genius. Blue, brilliant." Was I a writer? I'd published poems and stories only in college literary magazines, so felt I wasn't. "No." What did I do? I told him about teaching soldiers how to read and do long division. "Last year, I taught American literature for 'listening fees' in Heidelberg." He talked of Frankfurt as a beautiful city. In 1951, much of its beauty was rubble. We walked a few hundred yards up the road to an outdoor restaurant overlooking mountain streams plunging over boulders. That was beautiful.

Frau Mann seemed to be Chief of Staff. She ordered lunch for us, told him to put on his sweater, drove their car, made their travel arrangements, cut his hair; in short, she guarded the portals and the sacred *scriptor* behind them. He clearly liked it. I thought him unusually submissive and uxorious. We talked about a letter he'd gotten accusing him of being an American author. "And writing in English! I wrote back that my country was German, not Germany."

I said I'd read *Dr. Faustus* in English, but was having a difficult time reading it in German.

"It is difficult. Too difficult. I tried to stretch the language to its limits. You'll find my new story easier." (This was *The Black Swan,* about an old woman who mistakes a cancerous blood flow for the return of her period, and is undone by the false rejuvenation.)

When we shook hands goodbye, he took off his sunglasses. His own blue eyes were brilliant. I thought of the old mistress of Byron in James's *Aspern Papers,* who unveils her beautiful eyes to the idolatrous American narrator.

I wasn't idolatrous, but walking back to the train, I was drunk with excitement. Mann seemed warmer, kinder, simpler than his ironic narrators or the learned monsters they encounter. I told Marek I'd learned from those ninety minutes forty years ago.

"What?"

"The ease of conveying authority. When I said how remarkable his biblical scholarship was, he said it was illusory, and that a little went a long way in novels. 'Throw in a few guesses and you even look original.' He'd worked the scholarship up for the Joseph books, then forgot it."

Marek's publishing career had been made not by a Mann but by Robert Ludlum, nine of whose thrillers he'd published, first at Macmillan, then at World. It had given him his publishing clout. As for Delphinium, he'd have top designers, copy editors and printers, and Simon and Schuster would distribute. "So you'll have a beautiful book, and one I think we'll be able to sell. Until you came along, we were going to publish only new authors." The "we" referred to the two owners, who read all the manuscripts and took an active role in all decisions. That worried me a bit, but Marek said he'd do everything he could to see that I was happy.

I said that that sentence helped. I asked him what he looked for in books.

"Easy to spot, hard to describe. *Readability*. It's got to do with pace, drive. Roth has it." (I hadn't mentioned Roth to him.) "You have it."

"What about De Lillo?" I'd told him how much I liked *Libra*.

"He doesn't have it."

Well, okay, I thought, I disagree, but he's discriminating, and, more important, he's in back of me. I wasn't going to become rich anyway, it was a good meal, and he was a good fellow.

Ruth, who used to be sarcastic about my New York schedule— "So you've decided to spare us a few minutes"—was, to my amazement, waiting up in kimono and nightgown when I returned. "How was it?" (This is a terrible family tradition. My mother infuriated me on many a late-night return, and her mother had slapped her forty-year-old son Bert in the face when he returned late one night.)

"Fine. He's the son of the old music critic, George."

"Then he's related to us."

"No."

"Yes. Some kind of cousin. I think connected to the Bergs." Our father's cousins, the doctors Albert and Henry Berg, had been Daddy's idols. He'd wanted to be a doctor, but was considered "too skinny." That is, the Bergs thought he'd be incapable of climbing six flights of stairs many times a day to make house calls. Albert suggested he become what he—at first unhappily—became, a dentist. (The Bergs' names are remembered now as donors of the great manuscript collection of the New York Public Library.) "You going to sign with him?"

"I have. The dough's nothing, but Marek says he has great designers, copy editors and so on. Simon and Schuster will distribute."

"Now you're talking," said the loyal ex-employee who, exhausted now, kissed me and went to bed.

Tired of Julia's snarling, I read the second volume of Kissinger's memoirs, better written than the first, less burdened by histrionics, wittier, more relaxed and full of good quotes. (I like one of Marshal Pétain's speaking about the graduates of the *Grandes Écoles:* "They know everything. Unfortunately, they don't know anything else.")

Next morning, before going crosstown to Philip's, I suggested to Ruth that we go to the 4:00 showing of *Thelma and Louise,* a block and a half south on Second Avenue. She was delighted, which delighted me. We hadn't seen a movie together since we were children. (If I were forced to come up with the last one, I'd say it was *The Goldwyn Follies* in 1939, which we saw at Loew's Eighty-third Street, on Broadway. I remember Jack Benny's house tenor, Kenny Baker, singing the beautiful Gershwin song, the last one George wrote— "Love walked right in and stole the shadows away.")

In New York, I usually walk or take cabs. It had probably been twenty years since I'd taken the Seventy-second Street crosstown bus. It was a beautiful morning. The apartment houses, churches, synagogues, the avenues and streets looked peeled, renewed with clarity. For me, they were there twice, once in memory, once in their stone, brick and canopied flesh. Oddly, the bus riders too looked familiar, as if they were part of a permanent repertory company assigned to this route. In front of me sat an old Rembrandt lady in a black tam, a blue knit sweater, dark pants and rubber boots, talking to herself between swigs from a plastic thermos. Under her chin were layers of wattles—the complete works of an old lady.

At Lexington, a well-dressed woman of forty got on and sat in front of a square-jawed, white-haired man in a denim workshirt. From behind him, another well-dressed woman called to the first. "Beautiful pin. How's your son?"

"Elsa Peretti. Fine." She lifted a gold pendant for inspection.

"You look wonderful."

"You too. How's that apartment going?"

"Nothing yet."

"Don't forget us. We're moving them."

"Thanks."

"Any sales at the shop?"

"They don't even give *us* discounts anymore. It's the new software."

Woman Number One got up at Fifth Avenue. (She'd ridden three blocks.) Before the door opened, she flipped her ring and little finger at the other, who waved goodbye with four fingers. Each had tried and failed to make a quick score. The vignette of the reciprocal turndown had passed by the impassive old man. (Why not? It had been staged as if he didn't exist.) New York. I loved it.

Philip was in his studio on Seventy-ninth, a kitchen and a couple of rooms, purposely bedless so that pals won't be tempted by his habitual hospitality. Floor, desk and leather couch were piled with books, letters, manuscripts, notes. He was at work on another installment of Rothiana, that comic interplay of the self and its presentation, what we are, what we seem and pretend, how others see us, how we become or deny what they see, what is seeing, what is seeming, what is "is," and so on, central questions of modern thought and literature which he handles more wackily and profoundly than writers well-known for doing nothing but this. I sat down on the couch beside a Xerox of a case, Rosenbaum *v.* Rosenbaum, sent to him by Leon Wieseltier. (Rosenbaum One, Momma, was suing Rosenbaum Two, Son. Why? Because Son had a court order forbidding Momma from calling him "at all hours of the day and night to find out how I am.")

Philip didn't talk much about this book. It seemed odd to me. To some degree, writers are as secretive about their workshops as other people are about themselves, but Philip and I have been exceptionally open with each other about both. This book—which became *Operation Shylock*—called for secrecy. In the sunny room, among the piles of manuscripts, notes, letters and books, Philip looked a little like a one-man intelligence service, bound by some occult allegiance. (To a degree, it's every writer's situation.)

At noon we walked up Amsterdam to Barney Greengrass's deli-

Philip Roth and Richard Stern, Chicago, August 1990
(Photograph by Ross Miller)

catessen, between Eighty-sixth and Eighty-seventh. I wanted to have a corned beef sandwich there because Marion Magid and Norman Podhoretz, editing a story of mine for Commentary, had crossed out the "corned beef" my hero ordered from Barney Greengrass's, saying that the house staples were sturgeon and whitefish. "I don't think they even sell corned beef," said Marion. Since I hadn't been in the place for fifty years, I didn't challenge her. Till now. It was a great sandwich.

When Ruth and I walked over to *Thelma and Louise* in the rain, I held the umbrella, Ruth my arm. She walked very slowly. On the long ticket line, I asked, "Sure you're okay?"

"Fine. You?"

"A-One."

"I'll get you in at the senior rate."

I demurred, but, at the ticket window, bent my back and made gargling noises. It drew not only the cheaper ticket but the response from Ruth I wanted, suppressed hysteria, the mood of our fraternity. (In the hospital a month later, she imitated my performance for Roger.) I hadn't acted up in public for a long time. It was a little tribute to Ruth, and she took it that way. While there was still time, we were drawing closer together. That I should act in public as if we were alone meant we'd crossed a border: we'd assumed some of the freedom we had as children (freedom from other peoples' criticism, the often-resented freedom of the old).

Thelma and Louise was about a similar border-crossing. Two young women who'd been reined in for years take off on a vacation. Driven by suppressed anger, new insults and the intoxication of freedom, they go further and further until their final embrace as they plunge—literally—over a cliff.

Said Ruth, "I didn't like it."

"Why not?"

"It isn't realistic."

Her life was a long denial of wildness and impulse; she didn't care to see even fairytale versions of adventurous women. Thelma and Louise's final kiss and freeze-frame dive over the Grand Canyon mystified and annoyed her. Maybe if she hadn't been so near a much steeper cliff she'd have enjoyed it more. Maybe not. Ruth had never liked escape movies or TV shows. She escaped through the grit of her friends' lives and the psychological tension of good fiction.

That evening, the four R's—Ruth, Ralph, Roger and I—ate at an Italian place up the street on Second Avenue. Roger was amusing and interesting. I could see Ruth appreciate him, and appreciate my appreciation of him. For years she'd used me as an example to punish him. I'd been a good, dutiful student; Roger was kicked out of schools. I was cautious; Roger was careless. I saved money; he spent it. I defended him. "He goes his own way."

"Some way."

I once told Roger he should move out of his parents' apartment. He said he could handle them. I was relieved, but more so when he did get his own place, paid for out of his earnings as a scheduler at the Ninety-second Street YMHA.

Now there was no criticism from Ruth, only love, sometimes expressed by an "Oh, Rog," or a nudge to get his hair cut; she'd come to terms with his pace. There was much about him she admired, as well as loved: he was independent, he had a girlfriend, he took courses at Hunter toward his degree, he loved books and was what he'd always been, a charming person.

The next morning, Philip and I took a cab down to Murray Street. Three men who worked for him in Connecticut had come to install a Hunter fan ordered months ago from the only place in New York that carried it. When they took the fan out of the box it was missing one of its pickled oak blades, so we went downtown to get it. In a four-story brownstone, Leo Herschman had sold fans since 1932. The place was dark, boxes of fans obscured the windows. Philip managed to keep cool, though he reminded a genial black secretary about the antiquity of his order and the frequency of his calls about it. As for blowing his stack at Mr. Herschman, that would have been like hassling a wall. The old gentleman, in vest and shirt-sleeves, dug out the correct blade, accepted thanks and offered neither apology nor goodbye.

This part of Manhattan, brownstones, small stores, the shabby Roman grandeur of Foley Square, looks and feels as old as the Marais or Southwark. The new manicure parlors where Oriental girls wait to incarnadine the digits of noon customers suggest Bangkok. Next to one of them, a teenage boy sat behind cylindrical cartons of crazy-colored sherbert. Of a red, white, blue one, Philip said, "It's like eating the flag."

"The most popular," said the kid.

Another boy hustled out, ready to deal. "Anything you want?"

"Plenty, but nothing in sight."

"There's plenty out of sight. Name it."

What we wanted, banter, he was supplying. It wasn't coinable, but there was profit there (practice). That the two of them kept up with Philip, who's not exactly Joey Slow-Wit, suggested New York was in pretty good shape.

In a corner nut store, we sniffed a hundred bins of fragrant nibbles, exotic as a jungle. The proprietor, miffed at first, also made the best of it: two old snoopers admiring his place.

The next block was AT&T's fifty windowless stories broken only by steel mouths venting the interior gas.

We flagged a cab.

As we drove north along the piers, Philip described the new writing routine which removes the grip of literary celebrity from his throat: he recites the alphabet, repeats "Words, words, words"—"What I have"—and tells himself, "I'm free, I'm nineteen, I'm unpublished, I can write what I want." A few months ago, given an award at the National Arts Club, he quoted Kierkegaard ("Everything contradicts what I am") and said, "I'm not a writer, only someone who wanted to be a writer." (Hal Roach said that Harold Lloyd wasn't a comedian, only a "great actor" who played a comedian.) Writing had been murderous for him; now once again it was what it had been when he'd begun. Every day he stops at 1:30, and tries not to think about the book. He walks, swims, has lunch with Claire and does chores. Lately, he'd been driving to his friend Janet Hobhouse's grave and talking to her. (He told me Janet's history, the English father who deserted her, the Jewish sculptress mother who'd killed herself, her terrible post-Oxford marriage—punches and burned manuscripts—her good book on Gertrude Stein, two bad novels, her brilliance, beauty and sympathetic power; then cancer, a final affair—with Jeremy Irons—and death at forty-two.) "I tell her things I don't tell anyone. I ask her advice. And get it."

That Philip not only doesn't censor, but yields to and encourages, these irrational blips in what is otherwise an exceptionally rational character once surprised me. Used to them now, I think it has to do with the terrific strain and discipline of his life (the mouth which vents the inner gases). It's related to the nutty part of his fiction, the "craziness" of *The Great American Novel* and *The Breast,* the narrative caprice of *The Counterlife* and the truth-fiddling in the book he was working on now. I'd sometimes tried to rein in this part of him, luckily without success. My own nature and views are earthier, perhaps Wittgensteinian: the human intellect is too small to deal with most of the large questions it's somehow able to raise.

I reported the day to Ruth, then, in the mode of this summer, we talked about Grandma Veit (who died in 1933). In Cedarhurst—where we spent summers—she'd shared Ruth's room. "I hated it. She snored." My four-year-old self adored Grandma Veit. Her great blue eyes behind rimless eyeglasses, her long dresses and black, wide-brimmed straw hat, her wrinkled, large-nosed, beloved face was the image of benevolence directed at me. Not always wisely: she fed me sugar cubes in Schrafft's and dabbed her perfume stopper on my forehead till it was infected. (I bear the scar and worse, the edge of Ruth's resentment at being Grandma's pet.)

Back from downtown with a sack of groceries, Ralph said the Hungarian church down the block was serving a goulash supper. Maybe, but the church door was locked. We ate at a Greek diner on the corner, Ruth managing two bites of salad and barely making it back to the apartment where we watched a rerun of "L.A. Law," then talked more about our unillustrious dead, till an argument about Willie Rittenberg stopped us. I claimed Willie had been a New York City Council member, Ruth said I was crazy. "He was just a lawyer. A fixer." After a Yankee game, I'd taxied back through Harlem with him and Daddy. Tiny Willie boasted of property he owned in those awful streets. I wanted to but didn't ask why he hadn't improved them. (Perhaps the memory of his power translated into councillor-hood.)

Our argument beached recollection: we'd been dredging the past too conscientiously. Death was in Ruth's belly, that's what counted. Tomorrow she had a doctor's appointment; if things looked okay, she and Ralph would drive to their house in Southbury, Connecticut.

The next morning, we kissed goodbye. There were a few tears. We knew—who knows?—it might be the last time.

I walked to the Sutton Place apartment house my cousin Ruth's husband, Paul Tishman, had built sixty years ago, the first building terraced so that every apartment had a view of the East River.

Paul's collection of African art is one of the world's best. After seeing it at the Musée de l'Homme, Picasso invited them to Mougins; Ruth had called Jacqueline "Françoise," at which the old genius had laughed "like a madman." Their duplex penthouse was loaded with African beauty, but the downstairs was a little museum of Braques, Picassos, Klees, Miros and Lehmbruchs. I took pleasure in these icons of cousinly property. I'd always had this repellent trait to which I reacted with rage, mockery or laughter when it showed up in life or in Balzac, Proust, Dostoevsky and Dickens. (I'd written scenes of snobbish exposure myself, as usual keeping my own nose clean.) Although I had next to no desire to own valuable objects, propinquity to them meant more than aesthetic pleasure for me. There was the fact of ownership with its corollary that *no one else had it.* Beside the *insideness* of creation, ownership wasn't much; but it was something. Was snobbishness an element of my great affection for my cousin Ruth? Probably, as what excited it is probably an element of her great charm.

The oldest of my Aunt Hortense's three daughters by her first husband Sydney Worms, Ruth has none of her mother's harsh traits. Hortense, a blond charmer, was, like many American girls of her day, often called "Mary Pickford." Blonde—with help—till she died at ninety, she also stayed—without help—what my father, in the memoir my Ruth edited and had printed, called "pretentious."

> When she walked home from school with friends, instead of coming to our house, she would blithely enter the luxurious apartment house across the street as if she lived there, crossing over to our house when they had passed. She made us promise not to give her away, and to our credit we never did, probably because we were afraid of her. She had a terrible temper and was very strong.
>
> > *Reminiscences of a Gentle Man. Henry George Stern.*
> > *1887–1979,* p. 2.

My Ruth and I weren't afraid of Aunt Hort, but knew her temper. When I slid down her newly seeded lawn in New Rochelle, she hit the ceiling—but not me. The only time she lost her temper with us was when we beat her at casino. Then she complained or even

Grandpa Adolf Stern, Hortense Stern Worms and Ruth Tishman with Ellen, circa 1928

accused us of cheating. My parents forbade us to play with her. Our grandfather, Hortense's temper-tutor, also couldn't bear to lose at cards. He lost not only his temper but his friends, including Great-uncle Isaacs, whom he had cheated at pinochle for twenty years. One night he accused Isaacs of cheating him. That was the end. Grandpa never had another happy Sunday night. (An eighteen-year-old drummer boy in the Army of Virginia, Isaacs had been shot in the cheek. "Zuh bullet passed srough his mouse," said Grandpa. "Notchully, it wass open.")

Ruth Tishman and I kissed and hugged. Her shoulders were bent like paint rollers, but the face above them was still lovely, the dark blue eyes full of affection and alertness. "I just had an odd exchange on the telephone," she said. "A man asked for someone I didn't recognize. I said, "To whom do you wish to speak?" 'Did you say "whom"'? he said. 'Yes, I did.' 'I must have the wrong number.' "

A dear person. This was the way Sterns were supposed to get old. Ruth, at eighty-six, had all her marbles. (Aunt Hortense, Daddy and Aunt Florence had lost many of theirs, but they lived into their nineties.) My Ruth was only sixty-seven. Like me, she'd expected to hit ninety also.

Ruth and I kissed goodbye, I called my Ruth to see what the doctor had told her. "Good news," said Ralph. "The swelling in her stomach is fluid. He'll drain it later, and start her on chemo when we come back from Connecticut." Relieved, I spoke to her, thanking her for the good time we had. "I'll see you in August before I visit the Barons in Weekapaug."

After lunch with Jim Atlas, who'd done a Paris Review "Art of Fiction" interview with me and was now writing Bellow's biography, we walked over to his office at the *Times.* Three o'clock on a Friday afternoon, there was almost no one else around. I'd thought of asking Jim to introduce me to Rebecca Sinkler, an ex-student of Philip's at the University of Pennsylvania, the Review's editor-in-chief. The editor at Grove Press told me that a review of my book, *Noble Rot,* had been assigned, written, submitted, scheduled and never printed. (There's no literary silence as loud as that of the *Times.*) Best to ignore the exo-skeletal part of the writing life. The credo I'd tried—and tried and tried again—to live up to was Rilke's, that an artist shouldn't abandon "the living center" of his work to consider himself from the outside (even to enjoy his old work). When Bellow hoisted a champagne glass to "your Nobel" the morning he won his own, I loved the generosity but omitted it from the piece I wrote for the *Times Magazine.*

Yet here I am, fifteen years later, violating that silence, describing and boasting about it.

At the *Times* entrance, I flagged a cab. The cab's shield sported an Arabic name.

"What part of Africa you from?" I asked the thin black head.

"Why?"

"Curiosity. I've spent time in Africa."

"I'm not African."

I asked if he were an American Muslim.

He said American blacks were "soulless humanoid slaves," and that "so-called" Muslims were the worst.

"How about Jesse Jackson?"

"He'n Dinkens is worse. I slave in this cab to atone for the biggest mistake of my life: getting mixed up with an American black woman, who's about to have my son. American women won't cept their inferiority which Allah decrees."

"What if you'd been born a woman?"

"My soul is male."

"If you *had* been. Would you accept inferiority?"

"Why not? In the Sudan, women're treated as queens, be-*cause* they cept it."

"Is the Sudan such a hot model?"

"You been there?"

"No."

"I have. Many times. My roots is there. I was enlightened there, I spoke with angels at the Nile. And it's where I'm heading."

"To live?"

"To find women to breed superior beings."

"I thought Islam didn't believe in superior beings."

"That's Mohammed. He's only a prophet." Sixty-ninth and Third, my stop, he flicked the meter flag and pulled up to the curb. "Islam's older than Mohammed. It's the riginal religion."

"I thought it was based on my ancestors' religion."

"You're no Jew."

"No?"

"Real Jews live in Uganda. Merican Jews are Canaanites."

"I'll read up on that."

"The record's corrupt. Historians! Intellectuals! The Koran has a chapter against them."

"I better shape up."

"Glad to enlighten you. Have a good life."

In Ruth's apartment, I packed, checked telephone messages, then called my old friend Betty Fussell, who said she'd just finished her *History of Corn* (for Knopf), and was now doing a Princeton murder, her first fiction. My friend Paul, her ex-husband, was "still married to the Harriet," and about to publish a book called *Bad: The Dumbing of America.* ("He must be after a petal of the Bloom," I said. Allan Bloom's book had been a best-seller for months.) She said that Joyce Oates had telephoned her last year "to find out what you were like. I said you were okay. It didn't please her."

I told Betty I'd published some articles on a PEN Congress, the idea of which was to contrast writers in public with what you "knew" of them through their books. The page about Oates had so enraged her that she'd threatened to sue the journal in which it had appeared (*Critical Inquiry,* reprinted in *One Person and Another: On Writers and Writing* Baskerville, 1993) and requested they print a photograph— which she enclosed—to demonstrate the inaccuracy of my portrait. After more Oates letters to the editor, there was one to me asking to see the response she'd heard I'd written—it was thirty words long— and calling for "a truce." I wrote back explaining what I'd tried to do and said I hadn't meant to hurt her feelings.

Christopher called. We talked about him, me, his mother, Cathy, Alane, Nick and Kirsten, Andy and his girlfriends, Kate, Jeff, Liza and Alex, his four dead grandparents, his friends, mine, Ruth, Ralph, Roger, New York, Chicago, my work, his, our frustrations, defeats, hopes, plans. The works. I'd been talking to Christopher his whole life. His talk has enriched a lot of lives, including mine. Our difficulties these past years often have to do not with talk but writing, mine and his. (My "versions of him" have been troublesome.) Anyway, the four-hour call, the longest of my life, made up for not seeing him.

Chicago

$\mathcal{B}$etween June 22, when I returned to Chicago, and August 7, when I flew back to New York, there are only a dozen entries in my journal. In some of them, I can trace Ruth's decline: the fluid from the stomach is drained, but then there's more fluid; chemotherapy is abandoned; she's back in the hospital, feeling weaker; her veins are dried out, so they have to bore a hole near the collarbone to insert the I.V. tube. She's in a room with five others, one of whom plays the television at all hours and talks like a thug. "It's like a soap opera." Ralph is wearing down. Ruth tells me this, then he tells me. He thinks he needs counseling. He sees a life of invalidism. Chasms open around him: her condition, his own, money disappearing, help-lessness, hers, his.

Meanwhile, around Ruth's declining life, *life,* more or less as usual.

I went on writing a novel; Alane began teaching the summer quarter at the university; a new rug was delivered and laid down; a new refrigerator was delivered and installed (by a clone of the Chicago Bear lineman called "the Refrigerator"). Willie, the dour *flaneur* who does odd jobs on our street, came by in his immovable porkpie hat to borrow money. "My credit okay for fifteen bucks?"

I had lunch with Andy at the Art Institute, then looked at a series of identical gray panels signed On Kawara and dated. Not quite identical: the dates were different. (Ruth's pared-down life wasn't much smaller than this.)

I played tennis with my longtime partner Gary Becker. (His

mentor, friend, and—as of 1992—fellow Nobelist in economics, Milton Friedman, suggested that we organize a tournament of Becker victims.)

On the evening news, the death of Howard Nemerov. I'd spoken to him after his operation for throat cancer. He said he'd given up smoking and martinis. (For a few more panels?) Howard too had a sister, Diane Arbus. Twenty years ago, he and I went down to the Museum of Contemporary Art to see an exhibition of her photographs, photographs of—as Howard wrote in his *Journal of the Fictive Life*—"the perverse and queer (freaks, professional transvestites, strong men, tattooed men, the children of the very rich)." En masse, the midgets, giants, bearded ladies, human pincushions, albino sword-swallowers, a Seal Boy (hands growing out of his shoulders), a bare-breasted cellist, Ozzie and Harriet, Borges, Coretta Scott King and twins—lots of twins—created a special nation, an anti-nation, distant yet intimate. Howard, upset, said he had to leave: "They all look like our family."

Diane had said, "Everyone suffers from the limitation of being only one person." She'd first broken this limitation through Howard: "It was as if they'd passed through some secret experience together . . . They sat or stood, not looking at each other, but close as twins." (Later, she did it with her camera and her body. Her biographer says, "She told me she never turned down any man who asked her to bed . . . She told how she'd followed a dumpy middle-aged couple to their staid East Side apartment . . . [and] had sex with both of them.")

My guess is that the Nemerov brother and sister were as divided by rivalry as fused by love. In the *Journal,* Howard attacks her art, the camera's claim that reality is visible. Where language "asserts reality to be secret, invisible, a product of relations rather than things, the camera . . . wants everything exposed and developed . . . The camera wants to *know.*" Diane's photographs did *know,* while Howard's poems, for all their intelligence, knowledge, wit and lilt, didn't—even as they presumed to—or at least didn't know what they knew.

That night, head full of his locked, handsome face, I reread the *Journal.* "The only way out is the way through, just as you can only escape death by dying." Years ago, Diane had killed herself. Now Howard had escaped.

The next morning, Ruth called. "I'm back in the hospital. They're trying to get rid of the fluid. Dr. Caputo says it didn't form a good enough pocket. I'm as weak as a coat. I can't take the chemo anymore. Richard, I'm an old woman."

To shake off the gloom, I went to the Quadrangle Club for lunch and sat at the Round Table between my old friends Donald Lach, the historian, and Edward Levi, retired from decades of distinguished service (dean, provost and president of the University of Chicago, attorney general under President Ford, president of the American Academy of Arts and Sciences). Despite his decades of eminent achievement, Edward is fuller of self-doubt than Hamlet. As a young man he'd wanted to be a writer. (Some of his early stories and plays had been read over the radio by a teenage actor named Orson Welles.) He'd given that up and turned to law after an English professor at the University said that Anglo-Saxons wouldn't relish being taught *their* literature by Jews. A marvelous teacher, lawyer, administrator, he hadn't left a literary record, at least not much of one. Grandson of a rabbi whose tradition is that of the Book, surrounded by scholars who lived by publication, a true lover of literature, Edward—absurdly—felt diminished. Someone at the table mentioned happiness. Without dramatics, Edward said, "I've never been happy." (Of course, his—our—tradition doesn't rate happiness highly.)

After lunch, I ran into Allan Bloom, his chest and head swollen by steroids, which he took to combat Guillain-Barré syndrome which attacks nerve sheaths and used to be fatal. "I'm seventy percent recovered, but it can come back." Standing by the vine-covered fence around the tennis courts, Allan chain-smoked, lighting up with a long silver cube. He says, "Saul [Bellow] was my salvation. He was there every day. Sometimes I hallucinated. We watched a show on Jewish comedians. I hallucinated that I was the spirit of Jewish comedy." We talked about Saul's mellowing. Said Allan, "Maybe it's not so good for him as a writer. Though I loved *Bellarosa*." Cigarette in mouth, he waved at passing students. "How many of them know who Billy Rose was?"

"Chaucer needs footnotes."

Allan was working on a book about love. "I've dictated six hundred pages. Saul dislikes the style, says it's like the New Yorker when it shifted from the Talmud to *Fowler's English Usage.*"

"Dictation can do that."

"I'm a talker, not a writer like Saul or you."

"You going to teach this fall?"

"Saul and I are going to do the Brothers Manischewitz."

He died a year or so later, a few months after finishing his book.

That evening, Alane got a call from Robert MacDowell of Storyline Press. He loved her book and wanted to publish it next year.

Dreaming, I *heard* Mother's voice. It was there, real, as if she were alive, calling me. (Why not? If she were, the voice would have aroused an equivalent chemistry.) Still, since her death in 1978, I hadn't *heard* her. Something had unlocked the hippocampus (if that is where such memory is stored). I think it had to do with Ruth, or Alane, or even Bloom and Edward Levi. Mother was asking for *publication* too.

The next day, I spoke to Ralph. "Another grinding day," he said. "They're drawing fluid from Ruth. It comes from tumors." A blockage, either from tumors or adhesions, was developing in the colon. "Ruth's very weak. They take x-rays after every procedure. There's a portable x-ray. They bring it to her bed. Still, she jokes."

I called her in the hospital. She was feeling better. "I took a pain pill. Hope I don't become addicted."

"Treat yourself."

"Wish I could treat Ralph. I'm dragging him down."

"He loves you."

"I don't know what's happening to my body. I don't know what it's doing to me."

To *me!* To that her which is no longer *her.*

The next morning, Ralph calls again. He's in despair. "I think I need counseling." He dreads the future, sees himself unable to nurse Ruth. "The tubes, the shots, *everything.* And the cost of others doing it. I've made an appointment for the two of us with Dr. Caputo when you come Wednesday. I haven't really talked with him. I want to find out where we are. Maybe he'll open up if you're there."

"Has Ruth said she wants to die?"

"No."

"She's still Ruth."

"Yes."

"And you're still you. You've been wonderful, Ralph. Hang in there. I'll see you in a couple of days."

He said Nick had called Ruth. "Chris, too. And Andy wrote a nice letter. Howard and Adele ran into Philip, who asked about her. It means a lot to her."

Endgame. *Fin de partie.*

Some party.

New York, Weekapaug, New York

$\mathcal{A}$ugust 7. I left home at six A.M., walked to the Jeffrey Express, got off at Van Buren, caught the CTA train to O'Hare and was in Ruth's apartment at 12:45. In summer heat, Ralph and I walked past the old brownstones—ocher, gray—and the beautiful Magyar church, the oldest in New York, if not America. Would Ruth ever see it again? Outside the pavilions of New York Hospital, Seventieth Street was crowded with white and blue ambulances and ambulettes. "Ruth was ashamed to be in the wheelchair," said Ralph. We were in the hospital's oldest—1799—pavilion, the Lying-In. The "new"—1928—building was financed by nineteenth-century money, J. P. Morgan, Harkness, Laura Spelman Rockefeller. We walked up the curved driveway into its tiny lobby. The only decoration was a marble sculpture, leaves or phalluses; a botched Brancusi. I felt what I usually feel in a hospital, sunk. (Thirteen years ago I walked the summer streets of Fifth Avenue for daily visits to Mother dying in the Klingenstein Pavilion of Mount Sinai.)

Dr. Thomas Caputo is Chief of Obstetrical/Gynecological Surgery at New York Hospital. This should mean a magnificent office, but past a rat's nest of anterooms, a secretary here, a nurse there, there's only a small space made shapeless by its contents: walls of diplomas, certificates, degrees, black-and-white snapshots, tables, a piled desk, a wooden armchair, a beaten, leathery sofa.

Dr. Caputo doesn't look at home here. His real workplace is an operating room. This is not even his secondary work space: that's in the recovery rooms, corridors and nurses' stations where he prescribes, analyzes and talks to staff, families and patients about sickness, recovery and death.

No smiler, greeter, or PR man, Caputo looks serious. Bald, eyeglassed, his head sits a little forward on his short neck. He's fiftyish, gray at the temples. His voice and manner are economical, direct, nonpalliative, decent, the decency of a truthful, hardworking, experienced, undazzled professional who deals with the most serious matters without depersonalizing, abstracting or otherwise escaping from them. His gravity is natural, unpompous, unphony.

"I'm afraid we've done all that we can for Ruth."

The words hit Ralph in the middle of his head, widened his blue eyes. For me, they were a confirmation. Warmed that Dr. Caputo had used her first name, I felt that he cared about this person whom he had cut, drained, sewn.

"The episode with her breathing yesterday was the sign the tumors have reached the lungs. Her body is breaking down. What we have to decide now, before a catastrophic event, is whether or not to put her on a respirator. Once we do that, it is very difficult to get her off. We have to hear from her own lips whether she wants to be revived and put on one, or whether she agrees to be what we call DNR—Do Not Resuscitate."

Ralph managed to say, "You're telling us that nothing can be done for her?"

"No," said Caputo firmly. "I'm saying that we will continue to do everything possible to make her comfortable, to see that she has as little pain as possible. We can do that. But one of these days, her heart is going to give out, or something else will. She'll become comatose. This is what we must discuss. She could be kept technically alive, unless you and she decide that is not the way it should be. It is a terrible way."

Ralph seemed to be gasping for air, as if, despite the months and months of attendance at Ruth's decay, he'd entered a new element. "You know we've both made living wills. Neither of us wants to be kept alive that way."

"Even so," said Caputo, "I must hear it from her, now. People change their minds, and she can change her mind up to the last minute. I'm very sorry. I thought after the operation last year that we could get the primary tumor and catch the spread with a strong dose of radiation and chemotherapy. But she had this particularly lethal form of uterine cancer. It occurs in ten percent of the cases. Papillary serous adenoidal carcinomas. They are very aggressive. We managed to arrest it for a while. Then we had the bowel problem."

"And all the rest," said Ralph. "Stomach. Legs."

"Yes," said Caputo, nodding, remembering, disposing. "We could treat these, one after the other, the colon, the edema, but the tumors kept spreading, and now we face this decision. The two of you can talk with her about it. I'll talk with her as well. We can do it together if you'd like."

"I would like that," said Ralph. "Richard and I have an appointment upstairs with the psychiatrist in Ruth's room. Maybe he'll be able to help us with it."

"Good," said Caputo. He stood. "Nobody can tell when this event will occur. It could happen any time, or it could happen in a month, two months. It's impossible to say. I'm very sorry, Ruth's a fine person."

We shook hands. We thanked him for what he'd done for Ruth.

There were tears in Ralph's eyes. In the corridor, he said, "God damn it to hell. This is the first time he's said anything like this. Maybe because you were here."

"He said it because of the breathing problem yesterday. The sign the tumors had hit the lungs."

"God damn it. I don't know what to do."

I put my arm around him. "Let's go upstairs and see her before the psychiatrist comes."

In his shorts, sportshirt, long socks and shoes, Ralph looked as if he were going to the country instead of his wife's deathbed. His still boyish face, though gray, was smashed by anger, puzzlement, fear. (I myself was throbbing to Caputo's sentence of death.)

We walked down the ugly corridor to Ruth's room. She had a transparent plastic cone over her nose, a tube in her side. Since I'd seen her, a few weeks ago, she'd diminished tremendously. She was El Greco gaunt, her mostly black hair short, sparse, her nose huge in the reduced face, her arms stick-thin. Turning her head, she saw us and smiled, her black eyes shining. She took off the nose cone. "How wonderful to see you, darling. I'm so glad you came." She held out her arms. We hugged and kissed. "Hi, Ralphie darling." They kissed. "I'm feeling a little better. I had my fix." Her morphine. "I was reading." The *Times* and a book, Sue Miller's *Family Pictures,* were on the bed. "But I can't concentrate."

Ralph told her that the psychiatrist was coming. On that cue, a very tall man with light hair standing straight up on a long, stunned, bespectacled face stood at the door. "I'm Dr. French. Is this a good time to come in and talk?"

"Please come in," said Ruth.

Dr. French wore a black suit and dark blue tie. "Do you mind if I sit down? I have a bad back." I got out of the blue vinyl armchair by the bed and motioned him to it. "Do you mind if I put these in?" He took out two hearing-aid cylinders and inserted them in his ears. (I wondered if he were going to put in a pacemaker.) He looked at Ruth solemnly and said, "I've been asked to talk with you about your situation. I'm a psychiatrist with a Ph.D., but I also have an M.D. I've studied your records, and I know your medical situation. As you know, it's not a good one. I want to talk with you about it, see if you have any questions I can answer, any problems I can help you deal with."

Ruth said she appreciated that, and said that Ralph would like to talk to him also, it had been such a strain on him.

"Yes," said Dr. French. "It is very difficult for everybody. The immediate problem is this: the doctors have to hear from you whether or not, when a catastrophic event occurs—and that may come any time—you wish to be resuscitated. That is, whether you wish to be kept alive on a machine."

As this load of bricks fell on Ruth's head, I watched her eyes widen with terror. "Oh my God," she said. "I'm going to die."

I leapt to the bed, took her right hand and held it. Ralph took her left hand. "Ruthens," I said, "Dr. French means *when* it happens. It could happen a long time from now. It's just that they have to be prepared, to carry out your wishes."

Dr. French's bespectacled, moronic head nodded sagely. "They call such a patient a Code. You must decide now whether, if such a thing happens, as appears likely, you will not be in such a situation, because once you are on a respirator it is very difficult to take you off it."

Luckily, at this point Caputo came in. We told him what Dr. French had been saying, and he told Ruth, in his warmer, human way, that this was not a matter of immediate concern, it was just that if something should happen, they wanted to have her wishes on record so that they could respect them.

Voice trembling, she said, "But I went under yesterday, and you brought me back."

"That's right," said Caputo. "And we will again, if that happens. We're talking about something else."

I put in, "Like a heart attack, Ruthens. You'd be unconscious and then wouldn't be able to tell them your wishes. They just have to have it on record, now."

"I've made a living will."

"They just have to hear it from you, Ruthens, now, and you can change your mind at any time."

"I don't know if I can decide that now. Do I have time to think about it?"

"Of course you do," said Caputo, "But the sooner we know, the better. You can tell me tonight, tomorrow or the next day. Talk it over with Ralph and your brother. And remember, we're going to make you comfortable, you're not going to feel any pain. We'll do the very best for you."

"I know you will, Dr. Caputo." She took her hand out of mine and took his. His other hand enclosed hers. "I don't want to have artificial means used. I don't want to live on tubes."

"I didn't think you did, Ruth. It's a terrible thing. Now don't worry, I'll see you later, and we can talk more. And you can change your mind any time." He left, and she took my hand again. Dr. French asked if she had anything she'd like to talk with him about now.

"No, thank you," she said. "I don't think so. Thank you for coming in."

He got up and said, "I'll come back and talk with you. I'm here almost every day."

Ralph asked if he had a few minutes, he'd like to talk with him also, they could just go out in the hall, if that was okay. "Fine," said Dr. French. "I'll see you later," he said to Ruth.

Ruth said, "Goodbye."

I said, "Not exactly Sigmund Freud, is he?"

She turned toward me, a huge smile on her face. "But he's *gor*geous."

I nearly fell over, but instead patted her thin hair, its sparseness like Napoleon's or his Roman models'. Ruth was still Ruth, if not more Ruth than ever. "You're something," I said. "He's a creep."

"I liked him."

I laughed, she laughed, she was a flirtatious girl, relishing it and relishing my delight in it. Her neck was lined like a mudbank, her hands splotched with purple, her long fingers were clawlike, but she was delightful, teeth, lips, a crinkling, playful smile. The only sound in the room was the chug of the pleuro-vent machine clearing fluid from her lungs through a striated orange tube; another tube poured oxygen into her nose, another sugars and vitamins into her blood. They didn't alter the erotic playfulness, my appreciation of it, her appreciation of that.

She fingered an ice chip from a Styrofoam cup. Her mouth was always dry. The chips were all she could take; even sips of water gave her a stomachache and were vomited. More than anything she craved —like an Arabian princess—sherbet, but though doctors said, "Why not?" she threw it up painfully after three blissful bites. Now she sucked away at her chip with relief and pleasure—the gourmet delight of the last days.

What a trip, I thought, from the nutshell confines of the womb, through the years we call our life, to one narrow bed with one nutrient, the mind shackled by the body. (Though Ruth's mind, these dozen days before her death, often soared.)

I read to her, an op-ed column by James Reston on the feeble Democratic responses to Bush's mistakes. Like our parents, we remain basically Roosevelt liberals. Though I'd been somewhat altered by the skepticism—and research—of my conservative pals at Chicago, Ruth remained "pure," and her eyes shone with partisan relish. She smiled and nodded at Reston's points, made a fist and pounded the bed with it. I read her Anna Quindlen's column about a mother's joy when her little son showed how much he loved books. Right up Ruth's alley. She drew, fiercely, the boundary between television and books. Not once did she look at the small machine extended from the wall on its metal retraction gate like a Cyclopean peeper. What brought her happiness was a few paragraphs of *Family Pictures.* (Which is set in my own Chicago neighborhood. In fact, Miller's father, Professor Nichols, had died a few weeks earlier. I'd seen the notice in the *Times.*)

I asked her if she wanted me to read from it. She shook her head; she'd switched gears. "Did I do the right thing? What would you have done?"

"Just what you did, Ruthens. Live while you're you, refuse to be Code."

Then, tossing her little Roman emperor head: "I knew I vuzn't in duh best a helt—but *diss!*"

I loved it, loved her, loved the kick she was getting out of amusing me.

Nurses came in and out. A straw-haired trainee Ruth called "Ithaca"—she'd gone to Ithaca College—took her pulse. A kind, tough Brooklyn woman took her temperature with a cone that went in for a second and emerged with a digital reading. Others checked the centimeters of fluid in the pleuro-vent, her I.V. Everything was noted in the chart at the foot of the bed. Ruth relished being part of their lives, and she was someone they seemed to care for and to whom they spoke about their lives.

Ithaca asked her, "Is this your younger brother?"

Ruth pouted. She'd been passing herself off as my young sister for decades, not always that easy, although she still had the black hair of her youth (undyed, as far as I know) and, until the last months, a smooth face. I think she saw herself unchanged, full of self-deception. The pout, more comic imitation of disapproval than disapproval, was another sign of vivacity, her interest in the complexity of being herself.

Another thing Ruth cared about, and was proud of, was her memory. That too kept her herself. Like our mother, her model, rival, loving enemy and sometimes harmful friend, she was steeped in the details of hundreds of lives. Some of our arguments—we had them to the last day—were over who did what, when and to whom, who had what, who didn't. Memories were also the source of much of our happiness together. Ralph, Roger, Christopher would look on with amused superiority when we spiraled toward hysteria over our phrases, faces, events fifty years gone. No need to spell them out—all we had to do was touch each other's access key with a word.

An element in my fear of losing her was losing that. In the long history of humanity, only one person knew so much that I wanted to know. In the hospital, I primed that memorial pump again and again. "Ruthens, what were the names of the characters in Daddy's stories?"

"Idiosynchus," she said. "Alice Bobolink. And there was a running story about the Katzenjammer Kids."

The names were—are—in my core. Two years old, three, four, I'm in the right-hand corner of the room, I see the crib slats; Ruthie is in the dark across the way, Daddy somewhere between us. It's story time, the best part of the day. Alice Bobolink, Idiosynchus, Miss Demicapoulis (a midget adventuress).

Two months after Mother's death, I dreamed I was running across a green lawn towards a house in Cedarhurst, Long Island. As I run to Mother, I yell, "Momma, was I breast-fed?" Ruth steps in front, stops me. I wake up knowing I'll never get the answer. Where this dream came from, what it meant, I have no idea. I'd never asked myself was I breast-fed. I didn't—don't—give a damn. (I think.)

I told this dream to a few people, but for ten years not to Ruth. A few days before Christmas 1989, I had lunch with her in a coffee shop on Lexington Avenue. When I finished telling her, she said, "I was, you weren't."

What relief, what happiness. I had the answer from the only person alive who could have told me. Its rat-a-tat speed hinted at some important division of spoils which, for a change, had me getting the short end. In the dream, Ruth had stopped me, but by remembering it sixty years later, she'd given me something more important back.

Now we talked about Uncle Bert, another usurper of my mother's time, a man I found, almost from childhood, a foolish, ignorant, opinionated, immaculate fussbudget. He was always after me to be neat, to mind those sacred letters, 'p' and 'q', to have common sense. He disliked my politics, was puzzled by my love of books. Oddly I cared for, even enjoyed being with, him. (At some—early—point, bores become "characters." At a later point, I wrote about him, even using his name. I could not give up that monosyllabic chirp.) A cotton goods salesman, Bert was on the road nine months of the year. Home, he lived with Grandma Veit. Retired on annuities at fifty, he spent forty hours a week playing gin and bridge at the City Athletic Club twenty yards across Fifty-fourth Street from his hotel. A lousy cardplayer, a lousy golfer, he budgeted losses on the same sheet as the "turn-in" cost of his annual Packard. Until 1941, this car was driven by a chauffeur named Leonard Bernstein.

Momma had the use of the car and the chauffeur. Her sister, Irma, didn't. In the late thirties, Irma had died on an operating table. My mother blamed the doctor, but it was only now that I learned from Ruth that the doctor was Mettenleiter, the good friend of Irma's husband, Milton Sackerman. I told her something *she* didn't know. Mettenleiter, a refugee from Vienna, had once rented a room and lent money to a local art student named Adolf Hitler. After Irma's death, Milton and his two sons, Bertram and Richard, moved to the Hotel Brewster on Eighty-sixth Street. A fat little man with a bald cranium and huge blue eyes, Milton was a dress designer whose bad temper lost him one job after another. (He'd store up abuse, then punch the abusers.) I told Ruth again about visiting him in a tiny office in the garment district. "It had a drawing table covered with cardboard patterns, scissors, swatches, pencils, erasers, two chairs, a dirty, uncurtained window."

"I know," she said, smiling. "I remember "Wanderers." (A story I'd written about Milton and his sons.) "Did you know Bertram was schizophrenic?"

"No."

"He wrote about it."

"Where?"

"His autobiography."

"I didn't know one existed."

"He gave me the manuscript when I was at Simon and Schuster. It was marvelous. I showed it to people, but nothing came of it."

"What about Richard?" His specialty was train schedules.

"He lives in New Jersey, near Bert. Ralph and I ran into them once at Coney Island. Uncle Bert and I were the only ones in the family who treated them decently."

"Mother was nice to them."

"She was *terrible* to them."

Two weeks later, I said to Ralph, "Could we get hold of Bertram and Richard? They might come to Ruth's service." We couldn't.

Now and then Ruth dozed off, though her eyes stayed open, and she could snap to in a minute, sometimes correcting what had been said while she had seemed to be out of it. Still on top of things, she made some corrections scornfully.

At her bedside, the next day, I was telling Roger about our family's desiccated spirituality. "Your grandparents—our parents— were married by a rabbi, some sort of concession, though the rabbi was the most famously secular one in America, Stephen Wise, and the wedding wasn't at Temple but the Plaza. I don't think the concession was for Grandpa Stern."

"Yes it was," croaked Ruth, waking up. "That's why I was confirmed. And why you weren't bar-mitzvahed."

"I don't get that."

"He died when you were ten. Nobody else cared."

"I cared." (So ashamed of not being bar-mitzvahed, I hid out in the Paramount Theater all one Saturday, and on Monday, lied to my pal Eddie Meyer about the "closed family" ceremony, even gargling some phony Hebrew for him.)

"Maybe Bert cared."

"Bert? Baloney."

"He went to Temple every week."

If she'd said Bert's Packard had gone to Temple, it wouldn't have surprised me more. "He must have thought he was getting a price. On an eternal annuity."

"That's how much you know." And she slumped off, eyes wide open.

"Oh boy, Rog, if you'd known Bert. Rocks have more mystery in them. But maybe your mother's right."

"I am," came from Ruth; and off again.

I told Roger about my Grandpa Stern. He knew most of it, the red neckties, black suits, white moustache, the hominy grits, his calling ugly women "harpies," his temper, his love of Teddy Roosevelt, sending him neckties, finally getting a presidential letter of thanks, his books—some of which Roger inherited—*The Rise of the House of Rothschild, Of Human Bondage,* novels by Hugh Walpole and Warwick Deeping.

"Did he read Hebrew?"

"Daddy said he did. I don't remember Hebrew books."

"He read German," called Ruth.

"Did he go to Temple?" But she'd slid back to sleep.

"Grandpa sure loved him," said Roger, who'd read my father's memoir.

"More each year after his death. But he did, though Grandpa kicked him out of the house when he voted for Wilson, not Charles Evans Hughes." My father opened his first office on the ground floor of Grandpa's house. He was in his early twenties and looked like a teenager till he was thirty. He asked handsome, white-haired Grandpa to sit in the window, to attract patients. "Grandpa died in Florida in nineteen thirty-eight, when I was ten. Your mother and I went down with Daddy to see him off at Grand Central. A few weeks later, we were playing casino. He told us to stop playing. He said he was disappointed in us. A shock, he almost never criticized us. He told us we hadn't said anything to him about Grandpa's death. To this day, I'm sure it was the first I knew of it."

"You knew," said Ruth from non-sleep.

I was confirmed. You weren't bar-mitzvahed.

This was the second recent recovery of something that Ruth had been given which I hadn't. It felt odd because, if anything, my feeling had always been that I'd been given the big share of the life-pie. (Unlike Saul, who can still express the resentment at his sister Jane's having her own room—and way. "She got everything she wanted.") Even when Daddy blamed—and spanked—me for fights Ruth started, something in me felt favored. If I once resented it—I must have—I hadn't for years. (What does this internal whitewash say of me?) Have I squandered literary gold? When I went off to school in Chapel Hill, then to work in Indiana, Florida and, later, New York, then went to Harvard for an M.A. followed by three years in France and Germany, Ruth stayed at home, *stuck*. I married, had kids, got degrees, published stories, books. Ruth stood in place and, in my pity, seemed like the woman in Rilke's "A Woman's Destiny," "neither treasured nor special." I was "busy" and seldom thought about her, certainly didn't feel her near the center of my life, but when I did, I felt for her. I pitied her. (I drew on the feeling when I wrote a story called "Teeth" in 1961 or '62. It was the only time I knew I was writing about her. She said she loved the story, but I never said she was its source and don't know if she knew she was.)

The night of Dr. Caputo's declaration, Ralph and I met Roger and his girl Amy for supper at an Italian place on Second Avenue. The four of us drank wine, ate pasta and talked about Amy's life as a barmaid in London and a nanny in New York. Then Ralph told Roger that we had to talk to him about something. Amy walked home to their apartment, and Ralph told him what Dr. Caputo had said. Out on Second Avenue, they hugged each other—the first time in many years—then Roger walked back to his place and we crossed the street to ours.

The answering machine was full of the voices of Ruth's friends and relatives, Adele, Wilda, Doris and Bob Newman, Christopher and Kate. This electronic village was better in some ways than the flesh-and-blood support of a real village: a little abstract, but intense. There was no lingering, no prolonged farewell at the door. Message-leavers concentrated on what counted and got off the phone. The defect was the physical privation of abstraction: no hugging, kissing, handshaking, cheek-to-cheek warmth, tears.

So much of Ralph's business life was telephonic that, unlike me, he was at home with the instrument, a sort of virtuoso of it. My own expressive repertoire is narrowed by the phone, even in such extraordinary telephone talks as I've had with Christopher. (There have been times, though, when a single "Hello" over the phone—especially long-distance—has saved me from despair.)

Ralph made his calls, then I made mine—to Alane, the children and Philip. I read awhile, then, deeply tired, went to sleep early.

It was a bad night, broken by images of Ruth suffering, dying.

Ralph also had a bad night. The next morning, we walked around the apartment like zombies. When it was time to go to the hospital, I couldn't find my glasses. I searched every place I'd been, once, twice, three times, furious at myself and at this sign of decay. I found them in the pocket of my jacket, and went downstairs. In the lobby, Ralph remembered that he'd forgotten *his* glasses. When he came downstairs again, he'd forgotten his briefcase (full of papers about which he wanted to ask Ruth—bills, dividends).

Ralph said, "Where's the third stooge?"

Outside it was boiling, the heat glittered in the pavement and arced off cars into your eyes.

Said Ralph, "We should have put on sunglasses, sun block." (A ten-minute walk, Ruth dying, and we thought of skin cancer.)

She'd had a "good night." We told her who'd telephoned, what they'd said, and read her the mail. There was a letter from the octogenarian Spencer Klaw, her former boss at the Columbia Journalism Review. (Her last job.) His letter conjured up the office scene, Ruth keeping people in line, Jon Swan gabbing in Dutch and Spanish over the phone. Ruth treasured every word. The letter brought her to the edge of tears. "Such a marvelous man," she whispered.

Roger arrived and asked if he could be alone with her. Ralph and I went into the miserable corridor and watched patients attached to I.V.'s push walkers up and down the hall. Doctors, in teams, moved in and out of rooms. The place was a babble of nurses, therapists, aides, visitors. No recession here: sickness was booming.

Back in the room, I watched Ruth stroke Roger's head. They'd had a good talk. (He said she'd told him that she'd had a good life.) Now, too tired to speak sentences, she said single words, and pieced them out with her arms. Once in a while, her eyes rolled back and, mouth open, she'd sleep, briefly. Waking, seeing us, she'd smile.

Once, while she was sleeping, I spotted Dr. French walking the hall, up, down, and up again. He wasn't wearing his black undertaker's suit but a light blue one. (Was the black one for death announcements?) "I guess he's searching for someone to dump his load on," I said to Roger. (I'd filled him in on Dr. French.) He came into Ruth's room; apparently he couldn't locate anyone else. Standing tall, he boomed at her sleeping body, "How are we today?"

Mimicking sleep, I pointed at her. He finally got it. "I'll stop by later."

I said we were grateful for yesterday, but thought she was all right now, she understood the situation, he shouldn't trouble himself anymore. Words seemed to travel slowly into his consciousness, but when he finally got the message, he nodded and left. (Six weeks later, this two-minute appearance was billed as the second of "three visits" —the third was the talk with Ralph in the hall—"to Mrs. Leviton," the subject of the visits being described as "Adjustment disorder with mixed emotions: $260.")

When Ruth woke, we told her that we'd thanked Dr. French and told him that his services were no longer required. She said, "That was all right, but you should have said, 'She's sleeping, but she *would* like a kiss.'"

Dr. Caputo and his team were in the hall. Ruth said the four of us—Ralph was back—should sing "Cap the Knife," and she started croaking it when they came in, and waved her arms like Leonard Bernstein (the "real" one) to evoke our reluctant chorus.

Dr. Caputo and his team were not up to Leviton levity. He said that Ruth's left lung was filling, she needed a puncture and drain. "Is that okay, Ruth?"

Ruth shook her head left to right, *No,* but said, "I'm in your hands, Dr. Caputo. I'm not raising a fuss."

"She's going to surprise all of us," I said. "There's a lot of heart here."

"I know that," said Caputo.

The assistants' faces did not look hopeful, though one, a quite beautiful woman of thirty, seemed to me moved by Ruth. (Probably I was just moved by her.)

Twenty minutes later, a young doctor came in with the puncture and drainage equipment. He said to Roger, "Weren't you at PS 158?"

Roger, Ralph and Ruth with Kate, Chicago, The Point, 1980

Sure enough, they'd been classmates. Not only that, Ruth had been a good friend of his mother, who had—she told us when he left —killed herself a couple of years ago. (New York, I thought, the eight million stories.) He returned with two nurses and asked us if we'd step out. "I'm scared," said Ruth.

While they made another hole in her body, I went downstairs and walked half a block east to the overpass that hung over the FDR Drive. The Fifty-ninth Street cable car passed to Roosevelt Island, on whose high-rises were huge To Let signs. Garbage drifted in the East River. The only other moving thing was a tug heading for the Triboro Bridge. A new high-rise was being finished on Seventy-second Street; at its feet was a small café. Queens, Brooklyn, the bridges, the esplanade, the drive. Ruth's city. She'd never see it again.

The "procedure" took forty-five minutes. "Re-fixed," Ruth was feeling no pain. Now there were pleuro-vent machines on each side. Ithaca installed a new glucose sac.

I was struck again how much Ruth now looked like our Great Uncle Gus and Aunt Millie (as if she'd become our family Mount

Rushmore). The mere sight of Aunt Millie in her high black hat, the veil mercilessly pinned up instead of over her hawk's schnozzola and bemoled lip, brought Ruth and me to hysterics. "What's wrong?" Aunt Millie would ask, then, unenlightened, roar with us. Her husband, Uncle Herman, had run away from her twice, only to be fetched back from Chicago by my grandmother (Millie's younger sister). Herman was slightly nuts, he cackled in grocery stores and put eggs from the bin into his mouth. Luckily, they had no children. (Perhaps the cackling was for that.) The last time we saw her, in the fifties, was in "a home" in Riverdale. On the staircase, we heard her cawing about "the Pope's girlfriends." (She always had inside dope.) As always, we laughed like maniacs, and as always, it spurred her to further invention. That Ruth should look so much like her now was mind-boggling.

Ruth managed to talk a little, telling a story I didn't know, about helping Daddy pack for a vacation in Pinehurst. "He was joining Mother and Uncle Bert. He'd never packed. Grandpa always packed for him, then Mother." (In his memoir Daddy says the reason he'd had trouble with dental mechanics was that Grandpa never let him do anything with his hands, not even hammer a nail. "Go read a book," he'd tell him, taking the hammer away. When he went on his honeymoon, age thirty-three, Grandpa repacked his bag, and not only that, repacked Mother's.) "Daddy ran around in a state, not knowing where anything was or where to put it." She took a few breaths. "I was seven or eight, but I took over. Found things. Packed them. Got him off in time."

At six, I kissed her goodbye, and said I'd see her in a few days. I was going up to Weekapaug to stay with the Barons.

"Give my love to Kate, Jeff and the children. And have a good time. I loved having you here."

Back at the apartment—Ralph was having supper with his cousin, Anita—I called Christopher.

"I'll bet you're exhausted," he said.

"I am, but I'd love to have supper with you."

"I better not. I'm exhausted, too." His typewriter had broken;

he'd spent all day finding a new one, and he was still under the gun of a deadline. "Have a good time at the 'paug."

I went out for a bottle of wine and a sandwich, came back, watched the news, read a little and went to bed. At two o'clock, I woke up dense with feeling. The feeling was this: that for the first time since I was a little boy, I had a sister. That is, I knew what it was to have a person in the world uniquely allied to me, not a friend, not a lover, not a parent, not a child, something else: a special ally, no longer rivalrous, a feminine version of myself, an obverse side of myself and of my memory. This sister was special, far more than I'd realized. She was brave, gallant, very decent; she was a first-rate person.

I found a piece of paper and wrote, not to Ruth—I couldn't say such things to her—but to Ralph.

In the morning, before he was up, I left for Penn Station. The streets were mobbed, the station jammed. I waited on a long Amtrak line to get a round-trip ticket to Westerly, then called Ruth, who said that she'd had a wonderful day with me. Now she was reading *Family Pictures* and was happy. "Have a good time, dear."

I hadn't taken the train up the coast to Boston for twenty years or more. It—at least its successor—had taken a beating. The air conditioner above my head was leaking. I fed it sheets of the *Times*.

Again the familiar station names moved me: New Rochelle, Harrison, Cos Cob (the harbor filled with boats), Old Greenwich, Rowayton, Stamford (where my former father-in-law, John Clark, worked in what was then the tallest building in town. I spotted it among the new skyscrapers, a sand-colored dwarf looking as old as Knossos).

Kate was at the Westerly station. "I didn't bring Liza and Alex. I wanted to ask you about Ruth." I told her. She was shocked. "I had no idea it was so bad."

Twenty minutes later, we were on the beach, building castles, finding shells, flinging seaweed, riding waves. Liza, knocked for a loop by one, said, "I meant to do that—in part." Then it was back for spaghetti, corn, shrimp, wine, talk, stories. Gay, my ex-wife, who'd been there a week, said she planned to leave the next day.

"I hope you'll stay," I said.

"We'll see." (She saw, and stayed.)

After supper we called Ruth, who spoke to each of us. Then Philip called from Chicago, where he'd gone for his brother Sandy's prostate operation. He asked about Ruth and reported about Sandy. I told him as well as I could with the children nearby. "Terrible," he said. Sandy's operation had gone well. They felt close. "Our first thought was to keep it from our parents." (Who were dead.) "I said to Sandy, 'We used to be a box; now we're half a box.'"

I said, "I'm going to be a corner of a box. No box at all. A point." I described the decrepitude of the hospital.

Philip said he knew the hospital well. The summer before, he'd had his quadruple bypass there. (I'd forgotten. I'd called from the post office in Miélan—southwest France—as soon as I heard. By that time, he was home.)

"I'll be going back to New York Tuesday." I'd originally planned to go to his place in Connecticut.

"I knew you would. Hang in there."

After the children had been read to bed, Gay and I talked about operations, sickness and those we knew who were gone or going. Kate, then Jeff, then the two of us started laughing. Every word that hinted of illness or death—*tumor, operation,* even *bad for you*—touched us off.

The next day, every now and then, running on the beach with the children, or flopping in the waves, the sight of Ruth, tubes in her arms, side and nose, reaching for an ice chip, stabbed me. Liza reminded me of her. Her bright eyes—my mother's—and round cheeks—her own—were, like Ruth's, a stage for wit.

Alex knows when Liza's being funny. Though he may not follow the ins and outs, he laughs with her. I was Ruth's audience too.

There's nothing like the community of young siblings. Too little is written about it. Is it because early feelings are forgotten? My two-year-old niece and nephew, Joe and Emma Karlin, are often found by their parents laughing uproariously in their cribs. I suppose twinship is the closest society that exists. (As for identical twinship, that's

Nicholas Stern, Richard Stern, Jeff Baron with Kate Stern, Gay Clark Stern, Christopher Stern and Andrew Stern at wedding of Kate and Jeff, December 27, 1981

something between intimate society and multiple personality.) Ruth and I had less of a relationship than Liza and Alex or, for that matter, Kate and Chris, but even when we had least to do with each other, there was a force perhaps as fundamental, if as invisible, as gravity working away on us.

Jeff brought out a child's shirt. "Is this yours, Liza? Or Alex's?"

"Dad," said Liza, in exasperation, "why can't you tell whose shirt it is? What would you do if we were twins?"

I laughed, and Liza laughed at that—the artist's delight in the delight his art arouses. Had Ruth's early sallies drawn enough applause, or had my birth upstaged her? A little reductive, this: how many thousand—or trillion—moments, neurons, vitamins, bumps, smiles, rainstorms and whatever did it take to create a creator? Still Liza's seconds of delight couldn't hurt—could they?—and surely delighted me, their evoker.

I called Ralph at the hospital. Ruth was "up and down. They took one of the tubes out of her lungs."

75   A SISTERMONY

Liza and Alex Baron in Paris, Summer 1990

"That sounds good."
"But her back hurts. It takes two nurses to shift her."
"Can she talk to me?"
"They've just given her morphine. She's drifted off."

The next day Kate took Gay to the train. We kissed goodbye. I felt brotherly towards her, as if preparing a new outlet for such feeling. No, too much no-man's land between us: approaching it, we retreated, knowing the mines underneath. She was going to New York to stay with Christopher before returning to Chicago.

Jeff and I took the children to the Big Beach, a mile-long sand scimitar backed by dune grass. The water was weedy and the waves too big for the children, who hunted for shells. Jeff told me what I hadn't heard, that his great-uncles were in business with Louis Lepke of Murder, Inc. "Not in that *part* of the business. Still, when they told my grandfather—the youngest brother—someone was going to be found in a cement overcoat—and he was—he broke from them, changed his name from Bronowski to Baron, and didn't see them again." Brothers.

Back in New York, I left my bag with the doorman and walked to the hospital.

Ruth looked worse. She was more than gaunt—gaunt would be the equivalent of chubby—but she was sitting up. "Give me a hug, sweetheart." She held out stick arms. The purple-bruised, punctured skin was soft, the smile huge. Above her hung vinyl bags of fluid; on the floor chugging tanks drained other fluids. On the clothes cabinet a sunflower drooped. (A young woman, a patient, walking up and down the hall, had seen Ruth's smile and brought her the flower.)

Ruth couldn't talk much but liked hearing about Weekapaug. I also told her that Philip said Sandy Roth had a morphine pump. "He can give himself a shot when he wants one."

Ruth, grinning, pumped her arms like mad.

Dr. Caputo came in and said she was better than that morning, her pressure ninety over sixty instead of sixty over twenty. "And your temperature's back up." Still, fluid was coming into the lungs, the heart was stamping away, and they'd had to pull her back from the brink. He was putting Proventil in with the oxygen to dry out the lungs. "I'm going to give you something else to reduce the potassium, and another blood transfusion."

I followed Caputo out, and said I had tickets to go home the next day, but wouldn't if he thought I should stay.

"I could walk down to the office and she'd be gone by the time I got there. Or we could have this same conversation in three months. Her spirit's keeping her alive, and we don't know much about that. Go home. Do what you have to do."

I suppose some doctors raise curtains between their diagnostic ability and their feelings, and some just put them in cold storage. This wasn't Caputo's way. Like other good doctors I've been lucky to know, Caputo took on the weight of feeling; his brusqueness didn't hide that. I thanked him for all he'd done, and we shook hands goodly.

Ruth was floating in and out of consciousness. Occasionally she cried, "Oh, boy, oh, God," or made noises of relief. She wiggled her swollen purple feet, tried and failed to move her swollen legs. I saw them, because after Dr. Caputo's examination, they'd left her uncovered. I saw her nipple for the first time since God knows when. It looked pink, womanly, a tiny circle of health. But it wasn't right to be careless with her; I covered her. It was a rare lapse: the nurses were wonderful, performing the medical equivalent of last rites, changing the fluids, taking the temperature, adjusting the transparent mask over her nose.

When Ruth woke, her eyes were huge; she looked amazed to be in the world.

I said, "Gay's in town, do you want to see her?"

She almost yelled, "Yes. I *love* Gay." After a second, she said, "I also love Alane."

Roger: "She loves everyone."

I left a message for Gay on Chris's machine: "Ruth would love to see you if you have a chance."

Sometimes, when Ruth closed her eyes and we stopped talking, she'd say, "Keep talking. I like to hear your voice."

Ralph came in with a cup of fresh ice chips. Ruth seized it greedily, and put one to her dry lips. "If I could only have some sherbet."

"She had some this morning," said Ralph. "Hospital stuff. It's not bad. She threw it up."

"But I loved it," said Ruth, desperately.

She said she needed her fix, and Ann, a lovely black nurse, came in to give it to her. Before it took, she gripped our hands, then slid off, eyes closed.

I had dinner with Ralph and his old friend Cy Schimel. We met at Camelback and Central, on Second Avenue. Cy, powerful and bald, looks like Dr. Caputo. A great reader, his favorite writer is Isaac Singer. "There's a Greek coffee shop on Broadway, about Eighty-eighth Street. In the window there's an essay by Singer. I couldn't tear my eyes away from it. Even when you've read his stories five times they grip you."

It was a wonderful meal, trout, salad, good bread. I drank a bottle of white wine. It washed some of the awfulness from the day.

Ralph stopped at a fruit store to pick up oranges for breakfast. Waiting there, I felt dizzy. My eyes were heavy, there was a numbness in my foot and left leg. I had to hold on to Ralph the three blocks home. When I got there, I fell across the bed and conked out with the thought, "I'm going to beat Ruth to the barn."

When I woke in an hour or so, Ralph was on the phone talking to Adele, who said she wanted to drive down from Litchfield to give Ruth another shampoo and back rub.

The next morning, I carried my bag down to the hospital. Ruth, oxygen mask on her forehead, was sunk in misery. When she saw us, though, she smiled the enormous smile and flung out her arms for Ralph.

"My pal," he said.

"No," she said defiantly. "Your lover."

I kissed her too and told her I was going back to Chicago, I'd return in a few days. I read a couple of new letters to her. She fell in and out of sleep. Sometimes her eye blanked to the white, and it looked as if she'd fallen out of the world. Waking was sudden. "I don't feel well," she said. Her hands looked racoonlike.

When Ralph poked his head out the door, she said, "Don't go, Ralphie."

"I won't."

It was time for me to go. Ruth held out her arms and gave me a hug. "I love you," she said. I said it too. Then she said, "Goodbye, darling." I said that, too. Ralph and I hugged, the first time in our lives. I gave Ruth a last look, and she, looking, said, "I like it when you cry."

In the elevator, a woman was saying, "Children are the hardest to deal with."

I walked past the botched Brancusi to the driveway. There were no cabs, just ambulances and wheelchairs. Up on the FDR Drive a cab was discharging someone at the Helmsley Towers. I ran and caught it at the light. The driver said, "I saw you but thought you'd wait for the next cab. Thanks. Hard to get a fare, summer noontime." Was I from out of town? What was I doing in New York? I told him. He expressed his sympathy, then told me about his mother's twelve-year cancer, her death and his making up at her grave with his "hard-head Puerto Rican brother." "He fights with everyone, can't settle down. Me, I'm married thirty-five years." We got on the Triboro. "This bridge cost me a job."

"How so?"

"I was working for a supermarket, got engaged and borrowed the van to show her the Triboro. Who rolls up at the toll but my boss. Out of millions. He waves at me. When I get back, I apologize and he fires me."

"Son of a bitch," I did not say. The half-thought was aimed more at the driver than the boss. He thought I was paying for his life story, to divert me from my own. (I was taking it in, would remember it and, in the airport, wrote it down.) But I wanted to sink into one fact: out of Ruth's room, I was out of her life. Back there, Ralph was sitting by her bed, holding on to his papers for dear life, holding on while Ruth was in free fall, with no way out but morphine. Morphine was her papers, her cabbie, her plane.

Chicago, New York, Cornwall Bridge

*A*ugust 16. In the CTA from O'Hare I sat next to a neat, attractive woman holding a leather case in her lap. She asked me which stop was close to the Executive House. An auditor for Pier 1 Imports, she said that the recession was holding them back, they were opening only fifty new stores instead of a projected one hundred and fifty. She thinks and hopes that Bush can be beaten.

Larry Kart of the *Tribune* sent me a Thomas Bernhard novel to review: *The Loser,* a monologue about a good second-rate pianist nailed into second-rateness by a put-down from the great pianist, Glenn Gould. In the library, I went through ten or twelve books in English and German by and about Bernhard: *Concrete,* the rumination of a man fixed in the concrete of an ambition to write about Mendelssohn, recovering from a visit from his busy, forceful sister; *Wittgenstein's Neffe,* a more or less factual memoir of Bernhard's friendship with the philosopher's nephew Paul, a mad wastrel cousin of *Rameau's Nephew.* Bernhard works with the ashes of narrative, stirring and restirring them till his dull fury blazes. The German is clear, but the repetitious, punitive monotony of the chapter-long paragraphs makes for a sort of *Bad-Tempered Clavichord.*

In the heat, I played two exhausting sets with Ted Cohen. Ted, small, supple, thin, with top-heavy nose, dark hair and sometimes-beard, could pass for *Der Stürmer*'s Jew. Like all intelligent people, he uses what he has and makes it attractive. Ted is charming, reliable, omnivorous and as close to omniscient as a human being should be. For years, he's been one of my pillars: he's read everything I've written, remembers it, quotes it, laughs about it. Of course, he's also read everything else, remembers and quotes it as well, all part of his fluent mentality and gaiety. He's Chicago's central joke-bank, even teaches courses in jokes and games. He can play many, and knows the art and rules of many others. A natural athlete, he has the coordination, equilibrium and quickness of a fly. The drawback to a game with him is the depth of the conversational pool into which one plunges afterward, so tantalizing it's hard to swim to the less pleasant shore of one's work.

Four years ago, I'd played tennis with Ruth in Southbury. To my surprise, she hit everything back. I thought, "Steady. Reliable. Not much of a game, but not boring." Then, later, out of nowhere came a scream of rage, I think at Roger (or was it me?). I wondered if the scream were connected to the soft, rare game we'd played. Was there enough fraternal competition in it to unlock her rage?

Ralph called to say that they'd moved Ruth—and all the other patients of Lying-In—to the Whitney Pavilion. "Sixty years of decay, and they pick *now* to do repairs." Ruth had beshat herself, and was "mortified, but it shows her body's working. She also tore the NG out of her nose. Caputo said it was okay, said she could drink something. Her voice is better. I was the object of a little outbreak. She told Roger I was a fussbudget. Kate's coming to see her today."

I called later, while Kate was there, and talked to her and Ralph, then said "Hi" to a disoriented Ruth, who thought I'd been there in the morning. She said she'd see me tomorrow. I didn't disabuse her.

August 19. Kate's thirty-ninth birthday. "A big one," she said. She had nearly sliced off her finger cutting bread. (Kate has never been *chez elle* dispensing food.)

Hurricane Bob hit the outer islands of North Carolina and, at one hundred and fifteen miles per hour, was headed for eastern Long Island, Weekapaug and Providence. On the six A.M. news: Gorbachev "resigned because of ill health" and is confined to a Crimean vacation spa. There are tanks in Red Square and in front of the Parliament Building. Gorbachev's vice-president, Yanayev, is the titular head of an Emergency Committee. The other leaders are Kryuchkov of the KGB and Defense Minister Yazov. Yeltsin called for a general strike. Bush, in his sober, eyeglassed, World Statesman mode, spoke from Kennebunkport about these "extra-constitutional" steps, and said that the coup hadn't yet succeeded.

Spoke to Ralph. Ruth had broken out of morphine torpor to talk to Gay on the phone. Gay told her about Christopher's book, *Let the Seller Beware.* Ruth said she'd heard that phrase somewhere, and sank back into malaise.

The Tokyo stock market plunged six percent.

August 20. 10:10. Picked up tickets for New York. Ralph called to say the doctor—Caputo's assistant—had just said that Ruth would die in twenty-four to forty-eight hours. I called the children, then called Ralph back. He was in Ruth's room. "She's thrashing around, very restless, not very lucid." He asked her if she wanted to speak to me, I was in Chicago, but en route to New York. No, but she was glad I was coming.

So she's still herself, still aware. Very difficult to think of anything else. I get semi-flashes of her "thrashing," imagine what she's enduring. Not too endurable. Couldn't sleep.

Philip called, sympathetic, telling me to stay in Connecticut as long as possible "afterwards" for the relief, "which you can use."

Gary Becker came in for the weekend from the Cape. His brother phoned him that his house had lost only a couple of trees to the hurricane. We played yesterday, a great relief. Gary's the easiest person in the world to be with, sympathetic, modest, decent, his competitive fury banked when he plays me. (He wins ninety percent of the time, losing only when he's troubled or sees that I am.) Today I win.

Gorbachev is "recuperating" in the Crimea; ten pro-Yeltsin tanks stand in front of the Parliament; tanks of the octumvirate surround them. On "MacNeil-Lehrer," a youngish ex-KGBer (with a red toupee) suggested that Gorbachev might be behind "this poorly prepared coup." Coups, he said, usually occur on Friday; this one began on a Monday. Dimitri Simes didn't "qvite akree wiz zot."

Our rapid knowledge of events is almost simultaneous with (and, in a way, almost *ahead* of) events. Then they're drowned in interpretation. Millions of lives are up for grabs. There are deaths— amazingly few, a strange tribute to totalitarian decades—and who knows what will come of the death of that empire?

I'm reeling, either with fatigue, or tension, or eyestrain or— please God, not—a brain tumor. I don't want to leave my nest, though part of me *does* want to take off for woods, for Europe, anywhere. These are the last hours of existence of that person who has been and in a way will be, to my death and after, my sister.

Suddenly the word itself means something very special. It is a special thing to have had a sister, this sister.

August 21. Wednesday, 8:10 A.M. Chicago. Ralph called at seven. Ruth died forty minutes ago. She'd been comatose since yesterday, but the nurses thought she could hear. When Roger hugged her, he too thought she was aware of him, that she even kissed him back. When Ralph embraced her last night, he felt no response. He'd call Doris in Santa Fe to see when she could come in for the funeral, which could be Friday, if Doris could make it, or Sunday. "Saturday goes against the Jewish religion. And though I don't care," he said, "some people might be offended." I said I'd make a list of people to call and see him in a few hours.

I called the children, then headed for the airport. The early news is that the coup is over, the tanks are leaving, the coupistes are fleeing, or trying to flee, Yeltsin has asked the Russian Parliament for permission to block them. Apparently Kryuchkov, the sixty-seven-year-old—Ruth's age—KGBer, is organizing the retreat, as he may have organized the *putsch.*

A beautiful day, the first Ruth won't see.

On the train to O'Hare, I was full of Ruth, then what I'd say about her at the funeral, then what *Sistermony* would be like. Unlike sculpture, narrative doesn't work with single, crucial moments but with process: so I have to remember more than Ruth's generosity, loyalty, decency, public-spiritedness, modesty, love and grand laugh culminating in the bravery and dignity of her last weeks. I have to put down her fussiness, small-mindedness, indolence and harshness as well. A current Newsweek piece says that death is endurable but dying isn't. I wonder. Dying enabled Ruth to reveal a heroism and depth of feeling she'd never shown—or perhaps *had*—before; it also enabled Ralph to show a tenacity of devotion and affection he hadn't —as far as I know—shown. For one thing, he opened up to Roger, breaking free of the coldness, at least the distance, which was his own patrimony.

At the departure gate, a white-bearded Hassid in black suit and fedora peers over specs at a long printout of figures. (Why does it look wrong to me? I think I want his intensity to be used for the Torah.) The *Times* headline reads:

RESISTANCE TO SOVIET TAKEOVER GROWS AS
DEFIANT CROWDS RALLY FOR YELTSIN.

Inside are obituaries for Rep. Harley Staggers, eighty-four, who "worked to preserve the nation's rail systems," and a dentist-sculptor named Herbert Ferber whose last work is called "And the Bush Was Not Consumed." (Campaign slogan?)

A passerby with a blond beard looks at my *Times* and says, "There's no newspaper that's up-to-date with what's going on."

I think of Ruth dying as the Soviet Union dies. (The coup is the USSR's thrashing around.)

On the plane I sit next to a woman carrying a beautiful baby named William. (Hail, William. Farewell, Ruth.)

Ralph and Roger are at the apartment. I ask about Ruth's last moments. Ralph says, "A few days ago, she threw up her arms and called 'Enough.' It could have meant a lot of things. The last words I heard were when she was very restless, pulling at the blankets. She said, 'Quickly, quickly.' Maybe she wanted the nurses to help her."

(Or had she had a terrible flash that life had run out? Quickly, quickly.)

We taxi the dozen blocks to Campbell's funeral home with a roly-poly fiftyish driver whose shield reads "Jack Schulman." "You must be the last American Jewish cabbie in New York," said Ralph.

"There are two others," said Jack, who grabbed the opening to his routine. "What did the Puerto Rican fireman name his kids? José and Hose-B. Know why the Klu Klux Klan bought the rights to *Roots*? So they could show it backwards and have a happy ending."

In Campbell's sitting room we wait a few minutes—to get our mind on the expense of devotion?—till a bald, handsomely moustached, gray-suited man enters. "Bill Haygood. Please accept my condolence on your loss."

We're coatless, tieless and otherwise gaugeable as small spenders. Bill adapts his mood to ours and grows amiable and easy as we describe our funereal wants. We give him the names of my parents, Campbell's former clients, and say we want a similar service for Ruth. Flowers, yes, but not in vulgar abundance; music, yes, but not live, we'd supply a tape; no clergyman, we'd speak ourselves. There was the matter of transporting Ruth's body from the hospital, then the hearse to take her to the Westchester Hills Cemetery. Said Haygood, "There'll be another hearse going there from here Friday. Ira Gershwin's widow died yesterday in California, age ninety. She's being flown in today." In 1979, after reading the Twenty-third Psalm over my father's coffin, I'd wandered down the expensive slope and noticed the mausoleums of Gershwin, Billy Rose and Judy Holliday. (A few days later, driving in Mississippi en route to New Orleans, I heard "The Man I Love" on the radio and let myself cry.)

Haygood says death certificates are fifteen dollars apiece. "Banks will copy them, but you need originals as well." Ralph orders twenty-five. The death notice will be sent to the papers today.

HAYGOOD: How many people do you think might come?
RALPH: Perhaps thirty, maybe forty.
HAYGOOD: The Mayfair Room is available. Shall we take a look at it?

We take the elevator a flight up. The Mayfair Room has sofas, chairs, a lectern, flowering plants, even a coffin in which a waxy doll of an old man's head lies on what seems an unsustained suit of clothes. "You believe in realism," I say, "though it's not very realistic."

HAYGOOD: I'm afraid it's the real thing.

We go downstairs to see caskets.

HAYGOOD: The range is from $895 to $70,000. We sold the $79,000 one last week.
RALPH: A pity.

Roger picks out a gray pine model, $3800.
Back in the sitting room, Haygood totes up the bill. "$12,780."
Hearing this, I nearly give him another client. "How can the poor afford to die?"

HAYGOOD: Nobody has to go to a Potter's Field. There are many organizations, religious and otherwise, which help out. We help too. You'd be amazed at how many different groups there are. There's even one, the Jarvey Society, for indigent ex-philanthropists. It maintains them in small apartments and gives them a decent funeral.
I: We should have donated a few more bucks, Ralph.
HAYGOOD: Quite a few. Documented.

A great relief to be outside. We walk to the Rosedale Market on Lexington. Bob Newman comes out in his fish-stained apron, embraces us and says Doris will be flying in from Santa Fe tomorrow night. He'll get hold of Paul—his son, who runs a catering firm—and arrange the catering. (Which he—Bob—then paid for.) We go down the block to Melon's and have a couple of beers. It was here, after Mother's funeral service thirteen years earlier, that Doris unleashed her terrible account of the difference between our loving mother and her unloving one.

Back at the apartment, there were lots of messages. One said, "Call Bill Haygood." Ralph surfaced from this call, amused. "They added the bill wrong. It's only $8750."

"What a bargain. We could die every week."

"It's a great marketing ploy."

"Absolutely. It makes you feel they're doing it for nothing."

"He sounded genuinely contrite."

"That's why he can wear that beautiful suit."

We watched the news—Gorbachev was flying back to Moscow —then walked over to Fagiolini's on Second Avenue, a long place of wicker chairs and white tablecloths, full of people in straw boaters, bright vests and white pants. We got the only empty table, and had wine, veal, salad and *tirami-su.* Life bubbled up around the wreck. Ralph said, "I just can't believe it." (The classic pivot of our transformations.)

Only hours ago, Dr. Caputo's pretty resident had telephoned him. "Her vital signs are failing. Do you want to come right down?"

He'd hurried to dress, but minutes later there was another call. "She's gone." He walked to the hospital, kissed her goodbye, then "Got you the letter you wanted" (a doctor's note certifying a medical emergency to show at the airport). "I came back to call you and Roger, called a friend at Union Carbide and Doris, then got a call from Anita [his cousin] who'd heard about it from a friend of someone at Carbide." (The death network, the deathograph.)

We talked about what he'd do. "Rest. Maybe in Connecticut. Then there'll be the estate and financial stuff. Ruth took care of all that. I don't know anything."

"You know the accountant, the lawyer."

"I have the names."

"That's all you need."

"I don't want to do any more public relations. I like the work Ruth and I did for Lenox Hill, serving Thanksgiving dinner, things like that. Maybe I'll take courses at NYU, Hunter. I don't know. I haven't been alone for thirty years."

"You've got friends, Roger, us. You're not alone."

We planned the funeral, made lists of those to notify, those who'd be coming to the cemetery, those with cars, those who'd probably come back to the house. He was troubled about Ruth's things, clothes, family pictures. He wouldn't feel comfortable with them around the void she'd left. Would Kate want anything? "Ruth said she wanted to give her some jewelry."

"There's time for everything. Don't do anything quickly."

He showed me a clipping Ruth carried in her wallet, a short *Times* article about a literary award I'd won. She'd inked in the date, 4/16/85. I was surprised, then sad, wishing I'd given her more to cheer about, wishing she'd had her own clippings.

Adele telephoned to say that Philip had called to ask if they could drive me to his place after the funeral. She'd be in New York but Howard would be going back. We talked a few minutes about the loss, the unreality of it.

August 22. In the Times *was Ruth's obituary notice:*

LEVITON—Ruth S. On August 21, 1991. Wife of Ralph, Mother of Roger, Sister of Richard G. Stern of Chicago, Illinois. Service at Frank E. Campbell, 1076 Madison Avenue at 81st Street on Friday, 10:30 A.M. In lieu of flowers, contributions to the American Cancer Society or Lenox Hill Neighborhood Association would be appreciated.

On the front page was a picture of Gorbachev in a sweater, open shirt and jacket, back from the Crimea, behind him the stricken Raisa guiding their granddaughter. In another article, André Alepen, a twenty-five-year-old Muscovite, said the coup was not "fast and energetic" like a Latin American coup, but "a thick porridge, a Russian idiocy. We knew the Communists couldn't do anything right." R. W. Apple wrote about the rapidity with which electronic media had spread democratic ideas, "penetrating the stony Russian soil."

There was an obituary for the fine fiction writer and Mozart biographer Wolfgang Hildesheimer. In 1982, Hildesheimer had stopped writing. He said, "Literature is ceasing to exist or is already dead . . . everybody is too busy worrying how to survive." Before my hernia operation, I'd felt like quitting also. Now, after a good writing year, I felt that literature was flourishing along with me and would last till humanity threw in the towel.

There was black/Jewish/police trouble in Crown Heights, Brooklyn. A car in the cortege of the Chief Hassidic Rabbi strayed over the sidewalk and killed Gavin Cato, a seven-year-old black boy. Enraged thugs took to the street and killed Yankel Rosenbaum, a twenty-seven-year-old Australian Hassid scholar who was writing a book about the Holocaust. (Another literary death.) Trying to calm things, Mayor Dinkins was pelted with rocks.

At eleven, I took the bus crosstown to meet Christopher in front of Famous Dairy on Seventy-second Street west of Broadway. I'd read that this was Isaac Singer's favorite restaurant. In the restaurant last night, Ralph had told a story about a Jewish mourner trying to sell his services in a cemetery. *"Die ganze Tag bin ich mit die Töten wartend auf ein Lebendiger."* "All day I'm with the dead, waiting for a live one." The Yiddish (I gave it in German) which no one in my family spoke, for speaking it would have meant you were low-class, stirred up my need to be in Singer-land. (Cy Schimel had also spurred it.)

I got off at Broadway across from the Horn and Hardart Automat where, in the thirties, on Thursday, "Maid's Night Out," Daddy took Ruth and me (and, sometimes, Mother who "hated it") for the joys of slipping nickels into slots and getting more or less anything we wanted from the glass-doored caves. The Automat was long gone, but the look of the Upper Broadway crowd hadn't changed: gray-haired stogie-chompers, bent-backed ladies with canes, handbags and big hats. I asked an old geezer reading the *News* where Famous Dairy was. Without looking at me, he waved his hand across Broadway. "Kent miss't."

But I did, for a bit, going into Famous Cantonese Food, so I started to ask a big fellow leaning against a car where it was.

Christopher. He must have put on thirty pounds since I'd seen him; his front looked like a ski slope. We shook hands. He said, "You looked so much like your father wandering around, lost."

"You look great. A little big."

"I feel great. I finished the first half of the assignment yesterday, so I came down early and had breakfast here. It's terrible, but go in, take a look."

The Diner is dark, narrow, piss-colored. Wing fans stir the heat.

Few customers. A bald man in a yarmulka gobbled a pickle. I asked a weary waitress sitting at a counter stool if Sam Orenstein was around. Sam had served Singer meals for forty years. When Singer got the Nobel prize, he'd asked him if he'd be giving a larger tip. Singer replied that he'd like to give him one, but "My heart von't let me." The waitress pointed to a liver-spotted old fellow with gray hair carrying a bowl of barley soup.

I: Are you Sam?
S: I am. Who wants?
I: I've heard about you. Just wanted to shake hands.

He put down the soup, shook hands, picked the bowl up and brought it to the pickle gobbler.

I went back to Christopher. "You're right, it's awful. Singer paid through the nose for nostalgia."

Nostalgia was what I was after. Walking these streets with Christopher was wonderful. Our first stop was the Seventy-third Street Savings Bank where I'd come with Momma sixty years ago carrying a metal fortress slotted for pennies, nickels and dimes. The cashier would open it with the key, and I'd deposit the money or give it to Momma to buy me a present. The interior of the bank was still overwhelming. (When did banks put on such Roman airs?)

We walked by the Ansonia where Kate lived in a rat hole of a room for a year. Lillian Hellman told me that her grandmother had had a gorgeous suite there in the twenties. (She declined Kate's invitation to see what it looked like now.)

We passed familiar buildings, unfamiliar stores. "Familiar" meant that they were there in the thirties and forties. So the marquee of the old RKO Eighty-first Street Theater was familiar, but now it advertised not *Citizen Kane* but the meat market beneath it. At Eighty-second, we walked to West End to see PS 9.

Eighty-sixth Street, across from Singer's apartment building, was almost entirely—and to me painfully—new. Here had been that prince of delicatessens, the Tip Toe Inn, where my parents, Ruth and I came with friends or visiting relatives for brunch (though that word didn't exist in the thirties), most often with "Uncle" Edwin and

"Aunt" Bea (Mother's best friend). Uncle Edwin worked for a candy company and thought everyone smarter and more accomplished than he. The acme of intellectual brilliance was John Kieran of the radio show "Information, Please." Aunt Bea, weary of Edwin's Kieran eulogies, growled, "He knows books; you know gumdrops." Mother called Bea every morning at eight o'clock. One evening Bea told Mother not to call her the next morning. Mother held off till eleven, then called. A policeman answered and told her that Bea and Edwin had poisoned themselves.

Gone too from Broadway were the Yorktown and Stoddard theaters, where I'd seen most of the movies of my first twelve years, Ronald Colman in *Under Two Flags,* Gary Cooper and Ray Milland in *Beau Geste,* Jean Hersholt delivering the Dionne Quintuplets, Fred Astaire and Ginger Rogers in *Top Hat* and *Follow the Fleet.* I loved Ginger as intensely and secretively as I loved Barbara Felstein, by whose house on Eighty-second between Amsterdam and Columbus I walked every day after school. Once or twice she was there. We exchanged nods.

Chris and I looked into the lobby of the apartment building on Eighty-ninth and Broadway where Ruth and I lived till 1932. Nothing stirred. (Proust knew you couldn't squeeze much juice out of willed memory.)

We ate at a deli. (Chris took only coffee. There's a scene in *A Father's Words* about the son wolfing down an enormous meal; Chris was conscientious about contradicting and counteracting everything written about that character.) As we have for years now, we talked about his difficulties and sense of unrealization, discoveries made in his analysis and his withdrawal from them in his attempt to defeat his analyst. We talked about his brothers and sister and their difficulties, which he feels are much closer to his own than I do. He compared his mother to Ruth: "Ruth expressed everything; Mom suppressed it, though it came out in looks and gestures." As for *A Father's Words*— which supposedly kept him from speaking to me for a year and a half —he said now that "It gave me what I wanted, your mind, your attention."

I told him my surprise at how much Ruth meant to me. "I didn't think I was close to her." And saying this, I found myself—and let myself be seen by him—crying. He reached across the table and patted my hand. I could see that the tears moved and pleased him. Which moved, pleased and eased me. (Or was he acting—in part—as well? No end to these intricacies.)

"Would you like to see Cathy's pictures?" he asked. "She's doing wonderful work."

It meant another fifteen blocks, and my sciatic nerve was pinching my left leg, but after first saying "I better not," I said "Yes," and we walked up Broadway. Now and then I took his arm. It was important for me to have him know I relied on him, leaned on him. (I don't know his feelings about this.) Over the years, we've both felt let down by the other: I'd once refused to give him five thousand dollars in a lump sum, offering a part of it every month. I forget why he wanted it. And he'd once done nothing about a shipment of a Balinese sculpture I'd asked him to see about at a New York pier. (Ruth would have grumbled that as usual I'd mishandled things, but she would have gone down to the pier. I didn't ask her.)

He and Cathy lived at 108th off Amsterdam. I'd forgotten how grim and graceless, hot and small it was. The windows were barred, the furniture minimal; there was no décor. Two people of exceptional sensibility who adored beautiful things had lived here for years. What did it mean? It wasn't just a matter of money. I sat on a lumpy couch while Chris hauled Cathy's canvases out one by one. Cathy painted expertly in many styles. She'd also painted a series of bright vertical thrusts on fuliginous, unfigured backgrounds. I *read*—as well as looked at—them. They said what I guess lots of pictures say: "Leave me alone. Let me be."

The identical twin of another artist, Cathy had grown up in Cleveland, the daughter of a prosperous Jewish merchant. She'd lived in New York for years, supporting herself as a waitress (though I believe she accepted some money from her father). She used to work at the Plaza till two A.M. Chris would wait up to escort her from the taxi. Now she worked closer to home, still at night, and painted most of the daylight hours in the basement of the apartment house.

Chris wanted me to take one of the pictures. I said, "I want to buy one, I really love her work, but we have so little wall space, I'd better discuss it with Alane."

He walked me to Broadway, flagged a cab, helped me into it and said it had been a good day. "The best in a long time."

I said I thought so too. (After years of mistakes, I'd finally learned an ancient lesson—from Mencius—that a "gentleman" shouldn't teach—that is, "correct"—his own sons or he'd hear, "You teach by correcting, but you yourself are not correct.") We shook hands. "See you tomorrow morning."

August 23. Roger came over early, and the four of us—Kate had arrived the night before—taxied to Campbell's. Chris was in the lobby. "I've been here an hour. Lots of people are here."

The Mayfair Room was almost full. Joy, a pretty Hispanic woman, told the ushers to bring in more chairs. All over were people I hadn't seen in years, in decades, Wilda, Adele and her sister Norma (whom I'd dated forty-five years ago). We hugged as we'd never hugged in our lives. Words were unnecessary, but with more people coming in, we used them. I told Norma that she'd been the cause of one of my father's rare outbursts of anger. "Not at you. Me." He'd answered the phone one night, and a man from the Stork Club asked if this was Mr. Stern, he wanted to confirm "your reservation." My father hit the ceiling. "I've never been to the Stork Club, and I'll be damned if you're going on my money."

"So I lost out," said Norma.

"Years later I took someone else."

"So I lost out again," said Norma.

Doris came in, huge and mournful. We hugged and cried. Then Ruth Tishman, who didn't cry, and my uncle Howard's youngest daughter, Pat Cunane, whom I hadn't seen since Mother's funeral in 1978. With her came her sister Nancy O'Connell's son Tom Fitzgerald, whom I'd never met. I told him a little about his grandfather, my uncle Howard, who for him was remote as Moses. (My guess is he didn't know that Howard—and perhaps Moses—was Jewish.) Jeff's mother Margo came, and friends of Ruth of whom I'd only heard. The crowd overflowed into the hall.

Roger stopped the taped music, and Ralph went to the lectern with the pages he'd written the night before and gone over in the morning. Hands and voice trembling, he spoke of meeting Ruth on Fire Island thirty years ago. "I'd been a newspaper bum. Ruth saved me, gave me love." He couldn't speak the final sentences. Then I spoke about my surprise at discovering so much about Ruth in the last weeks of her life. "Hannah Arendt talked about 'the banality of evil,' a poor phrase and concept, but I'll borrow it to suggest that there's a banality of heroism. People who haven't been trained to be heroic, aren't expected to be and have never had occasion to be, suddenly act like heroes and heroines. It's what Ruth did. It was beautiful to see, amazing to see."

Then Wilda, standing at her seat, spoke about her lost lifetime friend, and Adele got up to say that Wilda had spoken for her.

More hugs, more talk, and we dribbled away to the street. It was boiling hot. Those driving to the cemetery lined their cars on the east side of Madison to wait for the hearse and limousine. I took off my jacket and walked with Chris, Kate, Ralph and Roger to Eighty-second, looking for the limo. Ralph said, "Campbell's misspelled the name on the death certificates."

"Wonderful," I said. "Subtract a thousand bucks."

"They'll change them."

"You'd think the goddamn limo would be waiting," I said. "All they do is arrange funerals. You think they'd get it right by now."

"It'll come," said Chris.

I went back to Campbell's with Roger. "Where's the limousine?"

"It's not there, sir?"

"No, it's not. And it's about a hundred degrees out there."

The man went into an office. I followed, repeating the question. Three men and Joy were there. They looked at each other, conferred, then a man spoke in a hoarse whisper on the phone. After a minute, he croaked, "I apologize to you, sir. I'm terribly sorry, but the limousine we expected hasn't arrived yet."

"Chauffeur gone to the races?"

"No, sir."

"Do you have another?"

"That's what I've been trying to get."

"All right," I said. "We'll ride in the hearse."

"I'm afraid that's against the law, sir. And there's no room."

"It's only thirty miles. We can walk."

"We'll do our best to send one as soon as we can. I'm terribly sorry."

"Indeed you are. Get the hearse. I assume you haven't forgotten that. We'll follow in the cars."

Ralph and Roger got in Cy Schimel's car. Chris, Kate and I got in the car of Wilda's son, Don Hammerman. Joy brought up the hearse, signaled the cars to follow and off we went uptown, through the Bronx and onto the Major Deegan Expressway, which was thicker with traffic than Russian porridge. Don said, "I've had the car five years, there's been no problem, but I'm going to have to shut off the AC or we're going to conk out."

"The Curse of the Campbells," said I.

"Easy, Dad," said Chris. "It's a New York thing."

To siphon off my heat, he asked Don—whom he knew—how things were going. Don's a professional photographer who does brochures for IBM and other big companies; he lives in Stamford with his wife and two children. An easygoing man and, despite his retching motor, amusingly articulate about hustling jobs, he brought down my temperature, if not the day's.

We finally made it off the expressway to the less crowded parkway. Joy lined up the cars at a center lane near Hastings-on-Hudson and gave us directions to the cemetery. We turned off into country, passed a huge CIBA-GEIGY plant, then drove through the iron gates of the cemetery. By the open mausoleum labeled "Gershwin" lay a casket covered with flowers. Poor Leonore, unattended. Up the driveway were Billy Rose, Judy Holliday, assorted Guggenheims and Lehmans.

We parked on the less prestigious upper slope near a headstone that read "Sackerman." Next to it, draped over my parents' stone and Ruth's coffin, was a square of filthy orange burlap. "What's this?" I asked Joy.

"That's the cemetery's responsibility," she said, but seeing my face, she went off to inquire about it.

Twenty-five or thirty of us stood awkwardly about rag and hole. I opened the Bible I'd brought and said, "Ruth wasn't a religious person, but I think she'd have been comforted by some words from the old Book which has made most of us much of what we are." The night before, I'd spent an hour looking through it. I'd found very few appropriate words. They were scattered through the last part of *Ecclesiastes,* starting with "To every thing there is a season, and a time to every purpose under heaven: A time to live, and a time to die . . ." As I read them, four workmen ambled over, removed the orange burlap and lowered the coffin into the grave. One of them knocked over a basket of flowers. I said, "A time to dig graves, and a time to knock over flowers. 'A time to weep, and a time to laugh. A time to mourn, and a time to dance . . . The heart of the wise is in the house of mourning . . . Better is the end of a thing than the beginning thereof . . . And when they shall be afraid of that which is high, then shall the dust return to the earth as it was: And the spirit' —I hope—'shall return to the God who gave it.' Goodbye, Ruth."

Ralph tossed in flowers, followed by Roger and everyone else. We went back to the cars; some who wouldn't be returning to the house said goodbye.

Joy appeared. "Your limousine is here." Sure enough, a wheeled palace pulled up, and Chris, Kate, Ralph, Roger and I got into it.

Bliss. Space. Coolness. Funereal luxe, but we were not funereal. Ralph talked about meeting Ruth on Fire Island—"Mousy Ed Koch was out there too"—dating her for a year or so, then worrying about marriage. "I couldn't afford it. I was living on a reporter's salary, a third of which went to my mother. I lived in a dinky room in the Village; I couldn't ask Ruth to share that. She said we could make it on two salaries. It went back and forth. Then one night she asked me to dinner to meet your folks. I came up to Central Park. There was a doorman, a big lobby, an elevator man. I went up to the tenth floor. Ruth opened the door, I took a look at the furniture, the grand piano, the rugs. We went in to dinner. I saw the plates, little silver spoons and forks I'd never seen before, and it was only the first course. I didn't know first courses. Your mother took up this little bell, tinkled it, and out came a *schvartze*. I said to myself, "There's a lot more to Ruth than I knew.' "

"You married my sister for the *schvartze!*"

Speculating on the lip of his wife's grave, Ralph said, "I guess I did."

Roger, whose existence was owed to that silver tinkle, laughed loudest of all. It was a merry ride. The Hudson glistened through the trees, there was little traffic. We drove down the West Side Highway. Across the river the Palisades gleamed; here were the George Washington Bridge, the Cloisters, Grant's Tomb; sailboats fluttered in the water, tugs churned it. Beautiful New York. Ruth's New York.

Chris said he had to work and asked the chauffeur to let him off at Ninety-first and Broadway. "On my street I can't be seen in a limo."

Paul's caterers had filled the apartment with sandwiches, salads, fruits, cakes, coffee and drinks. There were about thirty people there, which made it, despite the AC, hot. Kate got out the photograph albums: Ruth as a bright-eyed baby; a curly-headed two-year-old Ruth with two-year-old Doris and four-year-old Bob Lewin, playing on a green lawn; Ruth with black bangs on the back of a bicycle; Ruth standing bareheaded next to Mother in a stole and cloche hat beside me in a baby carriage; Ruth at eight, in a white dress, very pretty; Ruth and Adele playing ball, me in short pants and high white shoes running between them. There was a letter from "Aunt" Bunny on Camp Severance stationery. Wilda and Doris lit up, remembered their blue and white middies, the criticism sessions when campers pointed out each other's faults. Ruth had been hurt in those sessions. It was the first time I was aware that she could be hurt, and felt funny when she told me. She also told me dirty jokes. I remember only,

> *There was a dentist named Sloan*
> *Who worked on young ladies alone.*
> *One day in depravity*
> *He filled the wrong cavity,*
> *And oh, how his practice has grown.*

Chicago, New York, Cornwall Bridge   98

(And our dentist father? Never.)

Kate wanted to know why Ruth's middle name was Elinor, spelled with an 'i'.

I: We'll never know now.
DORIS: It's after Aunt Ella. It's my middle name, too.

Ella, my father's oldest sister, who said she'd be Daddy's mother after their mother died, and who, a month after Grandpa Stern brought his new wife home, assembled the other children and said they must now call their stepmother "Mother." Ella married the Mattress King, Ben Englander, and died young, about the time I was born.

Howard Goodkind said if we were going to beat the rush hour, it was time to go. I hugged Adele, Norma, Doris, Wilda and Kate, told Ralph and Roger to take care of each other and left with Howard.

There was no traffic, even on the Major Deegan Expressway. "What do you make of this, Howard?"

"Campbell's must be in charge of fuck-ups today."

The country became more and more beautiful. I'd been coming up to western Connecticut since 1952 to stay with Gay and the children, in the stone-and-timber lodge a wandering mason had built for her grandparents in 1900. (Cost: $800.) For the last twenty years, I'd been coming to see Philip in Cornwall Bridge.

We pulled into the driveway. Philip had just come off his treadmill and was wearing a blue-and-white knee brace. Howard stayed for wine and a concoction of Claire's, vegetable caviar and cheeseless cheese served on weightless wafers. Workout and exercise routines were exchanged: Howard canoed on the Bantam River, Philip and Claire were swimmers and walkers. Today, Philip had walked the six miles to Lake Waramaug in eighty-four minutes.

HOWARD: Do you think when you walk?
PHILIP: Yesterday, I zought, "M-Zee sqvared eqvals zree." Today, I zought, "Happy femmlies is all alike."

Claire Bloom and Philip Roth, Cornwall Bridge, Connecticut

He and Claire had just watched Gorbachev and Yeltsin give a joint press conference. "Yeltsin interrupted Gorbachev. 'Read the minutes.' It's all over. The Democrats should draft Gorbachev."

I went off and swam in the pool, managing six laps. Walking back to the house toward my pals, breathing the air through the birch trees, I yelled, "Life! Life!"

Saturday, August 22. A good sleep, though waking, I was full of Ruth. Or the fact that Ruth *wasn't*. Her body was in a four-thousand-dollar pine box under dead flowers and dirt. I'll never speak to her again. Roger can't call her from the office. Ralph's alone in the apartment.

I was in one of my favorite rooms: white curtains, white wood, an old stove, its black tube in the wall, a pine desk with a Xerox machine, a Czech poster of a nude, her huge nipple dark. Along the bed was a map of the Housatonic River Watershed, the river running south to Long Island Sound, the lake system around it (Candlewood, Zoar), with a hundred towns, Litchfield (the Goodkinds, Henry Ward Beecher and his sister, Harriet Stowe), Torrington (a tough Italian town), Kent (where Gay's uncle Fran, a state senator, used to live and where he and his brothers had gone to school, one or two of them at South Kent, where John Berryman had also gone), Warren, Cornwall, Canaan, Lakeville (the Hotchkiss School, Wanda Landowska, Kissinger), Washington (Arthur Miller and Inga Morath), Salisbury (which had a wonderful bookstore where Arthur Heiserman and I bought Mark Harris's *Wake Up, Stupid),* Millerton, Winsted (where Ralph Nader's father had had a restaurant). I heard a car come for Claire—who was to perform at the Mendelssohn Festival at Bard—then had breakfast with Philip, after which we drove to the Housatonic, parked the car, and took a walk in the woods along the river. Maple, wild cherry, locust, buttercups, daisies, flowers beyond my vocabulary; in the river, three kayaks, boys wearing blue-and-yellow helmets.

Philip's a stop-and-go walker, that is, a walk-and-talker. I like a steady, moderate pace. I just keep going, reeling him along on his word spool. He talked of certain—nameless here—human burrs in his life. "Maggie sends them to me." Maggie was the curse he married (the happy curse at the center of his early books). I have to force myself over Philip's scars and books to remember the small, solid, pretty blonde who baby-sat for and charmed us in the late fifties. At my thirtieth birthday party, we invited her and Philip separately, playing a disastrous Cupid role. (Though like a river, Maggie would have found her way to Philip somehow or another.) When they married and went to Iowa City, I saw them only occasionally, and though I saw him now and then in New York and England (in 1963), our real friendship didn't begin till shortly after she'd been killed in an automobile accident in Central Park. (The Maggie curse led to the way girls disposed of their underwear. Much could be learned therefrom: "For some, a pitchfork is too short; others you'd like to eat.")

We ate lunch at Freshfields in West Cornwall, sitting on the enclosed porch overlooking a rivulet and banks of flowers.

Back at the house, I did a dozen laps in the pool.

"Looking good," said Philip, who was doing leg exercises with orange ankle weights. We compared operation scars, my scimitar from rib to backbone, his zipper from collarbone to belly. (Surgical medals for what Montaigne called the practicing—*l'excertation*—for death.)

Dressing for the trip to Bard, Philip called in, "Gorbachev just resigned as head of the Communist party."

We picked up picnic stuff in Kent, then drove past white houses, streams, hills, cows and horses—the soft elegance of western Connecticut, eastern New York. Phil put on a tape of an old interview he'd done with Isaac Singer. "Wasn't I a good boy?" Sure enough, he'd asked Singer much that he knew more about than the old shrewdie. But Singer's canniness and wisdom, inextricable from his thick Yiddish English, were terrific. He spoke of the seven-year literary paralysis after he'd come to America. "I didn't know vot tings meant. Dot you could eat in a drugstore! Like combinink a bootcha vit a univoysity. Vich vun is it? Vot do you call it?"

Our picnic was with Norman and Sella Manea and Susie Rogers (daughter of our good friend, the novelist Tom Rogers). Claire was there for a bite before going to dress for the performance.

Norman, a writer who'd been in Ceaucescu's jails for years, was teaching East European and Holocaust literature at Bard. He'd recently published an article on my dead friend Mircea Eliade in the New Republic which shook me. It described Eliade's remarkable gifts as a scholar and writer but also quoted the mystic foolishness which underwrote the Fascism and anti-Semitism of the Iron Guard.

I'd had a similar experience with the septuagenarian Ezra Pound, whom I used to see once or twice a week in Venice in 1962 and '63. The intellectual filth of some of his views ground away beneath the admiration and affection I had for him. Pound, sardonic, cryptic, sometimes naive, self-doubting, apologetic, and Mircea, spirited, delightful, generous, witty, innocently boastful, were good to be with; I felt no mean fibrillation in their company. The relationship with Mircea was warm, humorous, frank; with Pound it was often silent but, once open, confessional, tragic. (The novel *Stitch* centered on this episode.) Should I ignore this actual experience because of these terrible old opinions? Yet Hitler, Goering, Himmler and Goebbels had charmed many people, some fell in love with them. Read the letters of Goering to his wife and daughter Edda in the last year of his life, and if you didn't know what he was and what he'd done, you'd melt in their tenderness. Serial killers were known for their charm, seducing victims to fatal rendezvous. Mircea and Pound were not killers, but their wilder speculations and literary power created an ambience for lesser and more vicious intelligence. (So John Kasper, the fomentor of the racial riot in the Little Rock of the 1950s, had been a disciple of Pound, and God knows what Mircea's early writing stirred up in the slime of Romanian racist nationalism. Indeed, five years after Mircea's death, his protégé and one-time literary executor, Prof. Ioan Culianu, was murdered in the University of Chicago Divinity School almost surely by creatures of that slime.)

I was puzzled about why I'd been blind to my own sister for most of her life. No wonder that historians debated the character and achievements of far more active and complex people. Revisionism? Almost any thoughtful person revises himself. Which didn't mean that every day you didn't have to put down the judicial foot. The law punishes deeds, not character, yet the deepest relationships are formed by character, not deeds. (Frigid personalities often do good deeds.)

The sun went down, the bugs came out, and we walked to the concert tent. Out came the brilliant Leon Botstein (a Schubert look-alike) to conduct the overture to *A Midsummer Night's Dream.* After intermission came *Antigone,* a monologue which—I learned from Botstein's program notes—had been popular until Wagner said that its music was "too symmetrical and decorative" to match Sophocles's intensity. Mendelssohn had been attracted to *Antigone* because "the play celebrated courage, love and a transcendent, perhaps universal sense of the priority of individuality and right over norms of power, fear, *raison d'état* and expediency." In my peculiar state, though, I interpreted the work as Mendelssohn's guilt-ridden tribute to his older sister, Fanny, whom he and his father had kept from a public career. Just before Felix composed *Antigone,* she'd returned from Italy and the happiest and free-est months of her life. As Antigone had sacrificed her life to her dead brother, so—thought I—had Fanny been sacrificed for her brother, lucky Felix. (I, a possible descendant of the Mendelssohns, was translating these fraternal stories into my own.) In May 1847, hearing that Fanny had died, Mendelssohn fell to the ground and, six months later, died.

I went to bed with the *Partisan Review* and read a piece about the last hours of Stalin (Beria kissing the conscious Stalin's hands, then, when Stalin drifted off, spitting into his face). Stalin woke and pointed to the painting of a lamb. Khrushchev believed Stalin was trying to say, "I am the lamb," but Svetlana thought her father was saying, "I'll do you as butchers do lambs."

"Isn't it beautiful?" Ruth said of the snow-capped alp, the only painting in her hospital room. Meaning, perhaps, *There's that too in the world.* Or, *If I were only there.*

Aftermath: Chicago

*C*hicago. August 27. Woke thinking of three sentences for Ruth's book, the first my own: "Modern America's 'scarlet letter' is black." The second and third I had to check and copy, the first Proust's, after Albertine's death: *"Que le jour est lent à mourir par ces soirs démesurés de l'été"* ("How slowly the day dies in these measureless summer evenings") and the other from an Italian book I was struggling to read, Franco Ferruci's *I Satelliti di Saturno: "Quella estate si mostra gremita di addensamenti revelatori"* ("This summer is thick with dense revelations").

I read Bossuet's funeral oration for Henriette of France in a book bought in 1949, after Alain de Grainville (with whom I exchanged English for French lessons at the Pension Marie Antoinette) told me that Bossuet wrote "the purest French ever written." Too grand for Ruth.

Ralph called. He said that mornings are the worst: the emptiness of the bed, the room. Ruth Tishman had come to the house after I'd left, looked over the albums with Doris, then said that she was sorry she hadn't known Ruth better: "She was much younger than I." This upset Ralph.

I reread my journals to find out the sequence of Ruth's illness. The first notice was on April 7, 1990, when she called to say that she had cervical cancer. I didn't record my reaction.

April 19. Ruth said she'd have her surgery next Tuesday. She hated the CT scan; had to drink cranberry juice and iodine, and was still getting rid of it.

There was nothing else of note about Ruth till November 24th. She'd visited Kate and Jeff in Bethesda. They had colds, and she and Ralph sat outside because of her low white corpuscle count.

January 5, 1991. *I called Ruth for her birthday. More radiation treatment. But she sounds cheerful. She and Ralph are thinking of taking Philip's course at Hunter.*

March 23. *Ralph called. A bad week. The chemotherapy thickened the walls of the intestine. There's a blockage which needs opening. Spoke to her. She always sounds cheerier than you expect her to. I find my feelings for her stronger than ever.*

March 25. *Ralph just called. Ruth's intestine is blocked and she needs surgery. I find myself in a heightened, tense state about Ruth. Twice I've tried to call her hospital room and been told, "The number you have called has been restricted from receiving incoming calls."*

March 26. *Reason I couldn't get through to Ruth: Ralph fucked up the number. Got through at 9:30, she was trembly, fearful. I reassured her, and she kept saying, "I hope so." Said she can't concentrate on anything but "the body."*
Ralph called late. The operation's much more serious, not just adhesions in the colon, but something else. Her blood count suggests tumors. She might have to have a colostomy if they can't resect the bowel. She overheard Ralph and the doctor talking about that and was terrified. A cardiologist will be present, as she had a small heart attack during the last operation. She never told me!

Wednesday, March 27. *10:20. The operation "went well." Two bypasses, colon and intestine, no colostomy, but the second blockage is tumor-related, and she can't take more radiation. The surgeon said she must be built up, "And then we'll see."*
3:45. Ralph called. Ruth cheerful, walked a few steps, then exhausted. Less cheerful when morphine wears off. Dr. Caputo said the original uterine papillary tumor—not a lymphoma, mother's cancer—was deep, and the heavy dose of radiation and chemotherapy didn't eliminate it. The tumors are there, small and

*spreading. Ruth doesn't know. Ralph told Roger: "Though I
shouldn't have, he has exams tonight, but I had to tell somebody.
There was a seder in the hospital today. They wanted to recruit
me."*

Alane is worried about me. I said, "I don't have a uterus."

March 28. *9:45. Got supply of new checks from the bank and
wondered if Ruth would be alive when they were used up.
4:50. Couldn't work. Drinking burgundy. Talked to Ruth. She's
feeling a little better. She's in a room with three other patients,
one of whom uses the phone till one AM and browbeats everyone.
"A criminal type. The doctor had to read the riot act to her.
Yesterday she talked to a longshoreman. I can't sleep anyway. I
enjoy the soap-opera aspect of it."*

"Are you in much pain?"

"I've never had anything like this. I hope this is it."

*Adele, Wilda and Doris call every day. She's angry at Chris. He'd
promised to visit her, bring her flowers, walk with her in the park.
"And nothing." Her nurse is a tyrant, a "General Schwarzkopf,"
meaning tough. Ruth asked her, "Why do you have to be so
nasty?" This apparently helped.*

*Ruth still doesn't know how serious the trouble is.
(Who does? Why are we made this way?)*

*Lunch at Round Table. How comfortable I am with these old pals
I see only at lunch, mostly old guys not yet peeled off the world,
glued here at noon to our table, talking of Schwarzkopf, a new
biog of Nixon, Gerald Ford as seen at cabinet meetings by
Edward, Caro's Lyndon Johnson.*

*Called all the children and Ruth, who was very sweet about the
flowers, but tired and weak.*

*Alane and I with Saul and Janis to Siam. Saul's new game: Bad
Presents: the Medusa Shampoo, the Lady Macbeth Hand Lotion.
On E.S.: "He controls the world with his tight ass. If he ever lets
go of the sphincter muscle, we're all lost." On a prolific writer:
"It's said she's a split personality, both halves with typewriters."
Cold, Saul put on Janis's scarf and did a shuffle-step to the
Eastern muzak.*

10:30. Ralph called. Another setback. Ruth's swollen leg very bothersome. They suspected blockage, took x-rays. "One positive note—she was so scared she shat . . . which humiliated and depressed her, but at least she's functioning."

April 3. Noon. Back from a rare victory over Gary. Driving to courts, swerving around a mattress dumped into the middle of 55th St. Gary: Guess they couldn't wait. Accepted Shulamit Ran's invitation to do a program with her before a Chicago Symphony concert. She's their Composer-in-Residence, reading scores from all over the world and interviewing composers. (When can she compose?)

Graham Greene, eighty-six, died this morning in Geneva. A bad week for Grahams. Martha died three days ago. (She and I had one good talk, back at Connecticut College in 1954 about Susanne Langer's Feeling and Form, which we both thought terrific. She talked as she danced, fluently and surprisingly.)

Ruth developed another leg clot, then a knot of bloody tissue on her stomach. She—and Ralph too—are wearing down.

April 4. Ruth very low, very sweet. The blood thinner's giving her trouble. Last night the IV started bleeding. The doctors clustered around her a long time. The surgery is like a bombardment, some of the consequences are unpredictable. (The Kurds have just been bombed out of Kirkuk and are dying in the snowy mountains, cursing Bush, whom, weeks ago, they called "Hadji Bush.")

At lunch I said, "Why didn't God make us of sterner stuff?" Jock Weintraub: "Have you made the most of what's there?"

Sent Liza a postcard of that beautiful, sad winter scene of the elder Breughel, ice-skaters, birds, huntsmen, no faces showing.

April 11. Ralph called last night, very low, Ruth wearing down; he doesn't think there's much hope. He'll ask Dr. Caputo the hard questions today, in preparation for telling Ruth, who must be told because she must be given chemotherapy. I called her this morning. She's overcome by lethargy, discomfort, is very unhappy, can't talk much. Last night fear and pity for her fused with fear for myself, felt in that center of fear, the bowels. (Was it partially

*the effect of the tetanus shot and antibiotic the doctor in
Emergency gave me two nights ago, when I banged my hand on a
rusty nail on the basement door to prepare for the coming of three
new bookcases? Saying* timor mortis conturbat me *over and over
helped, the Latin somehow making something special of the fear.
Yet the fear was deeper than it's ever been. I want to live long,
but may well—Ruth's genes are also mine—not live as long as
I've counted on. Talking about death is one thing,* feeling *it
something else. Shakespeare's "brave men dying once" doesn't
work for me. You've got to swallow terror, and deal with its
humiliating physiology. Not easy. Ruthens, picking up on my
"Hang in there," knows it. A sweet, brave try in the midst of her
unhappiness and weakness.*

April 12. *Roosevelt's death day, forty-six years ago, also, I think, a
Friday. Overwhelmed, I went to a typewriter in the* Daily Tar
Heel *office and, in tears, wrote a tribute. (I don't remember
whether it got into the paper or not.) In New York, Ruth and
Mother whispered about it, saying, "Let's not tell Dad till after
dinner." Hearing them, thinking something had happened to me,
he leapt up and interrogated them. So the news of his beloved
Roosevelt's death was initially a relief.*
*Philip called, said he'd run into Susan Glassman, told Saul on the
phone, "I ran into one of your ex-wives the other day." Saul:
"That's like running into a panhandler on the subway."*
*Phil adores Miami, the liveliness of the Cubans—"They're like
Jews"—the beautiful reclaimed Art Deco hotels, the old Jews, the
whorish outfits of the eighteen-year-old Jewish granddaughters.
"I'd like to dip their cunts in cocktail sauce."*
*Last night I called weary Ralph. They're going to tell Ruth today
about her cancer, the "aggressive" papillary serous cells. He'll call
me about her reaction.*

April 14. *Spoke with Ruth, the day after Ralph told her that the
cancer was still in her. She'd cried, they'd cried, then talked and
calmed down. She said, "It's really something, isn't it?"
"Yes," I said. "You're still only a little girl." And, "It goes so
quickly." And so on, with tears, and a sweetness of sympathy,*

*unlike anything we've ever had. She said Nick had written and
called. He's her favorite because of his sweetness—"Like Roger."
Alane, in her Sunday call home, learned that Janet and Peter (her
sister and her fiancé) are planning a trip to Vietnam. Alane:
"What's in Vietnam?" Harry (her father): "Dogs trying not to be
meals."*

April 27. *11:45. Ruth says her legs are almost back to normal, but "I
feel what mother called* schwach *[weak]." She'd been outside for
a few minutes with Amanda Gomez, her nurse's aide. Philip called
after getting his Brandeis degree. The attraction was Harry
Belafonte, to the disgust of Daniel Bell (who told fifteen Jewish
jokes). Then Phil and Claire drove to Updike's mansion in the
woods overlooking the Atlantic. U, in chinos and sneakers, didn't
know where to sit. Martha, a psychiatric social worker, came
home and they had chicken salad with grapes. No wine—U can't
drink because of psoriasis, and had forgotten it was a holiday, so
couldn't buy any for them. Three times he asked P if he wanted to
see "where I work." "Which means 'live,'" said Phil. They went
up to four tiny attic rooms, books and galleys everywhere, pictures
of parents, himself, himself with Saul (U: "I know he hates my
work, but I love his"), an old word processor. U was wry, very
funny, has pink skin with the little marks of his disease. Martha
was discomfited by the bit in* Self-Consciousness *about U
masturbating the neighbors' wives as they were "entering Ipswich."
"The imp of the perverse. Just like me," said P. Philip's staggered
by U's fluency and mastery. [For me,* Rabbit at Rest *is a
masterpiece,* The Coup, *about fifty stories and* Hugging the
Shore *marvelous. [sic] Odd Jobs as well. I also liked* Brazil.
*There are also wonderful sections, particularly the first sixty pages
of* Rabbit Redux. *A .330 hitter. That's Hall of Fame.]
Reproducing family pictures for the children. I'll take Kate and
Christopher's east when I go to see them and Ruth.*

This was every journal entry in which Ruth was mentioned
before the first trip east in June. Now back in Chicago, after her
death, more or less normal life resumed, except that I put aside a

novel and began full-time work on this book. ("Full-time" in the sense of my thirty-six-year University of Chicago routine, which Norman Maclean* and Walter Blair helped me establish when I came in 1955, writing in the morning, doing my university work in the afternoon.)

Although I'd done a few books of non-fiction, this would be the first not made up of individual pieces. How to do it? Just (!) put down what I remember, as if I were photographing thoughts, then snip, splice, paste and wipe out paste marks; maybe some *post hoc* photography, as memory brings things up from the well. Used to the freedom of fiction, I'm unsure about actuality. All this life, yes, but where's the shape? Is part of the point to record the shagginess of life around Ruth's dying? I wish the sistermony would include some tips about writing it.

On September 4th I wrote, *Two weeks ago this morning Ruth died. It seems like two years. So much l-i-f-e has 'happened' since; she's already missed so much.*

Why is love withheld—suppressed, unexpressed? Is it like electricity, too powerful to release without insulation?

September 9. I found an undated letter from Ruth written on New York Hospital stationery. She worked there with a woman doctor, whose name, I think, was Polly.

Dear Rich,

Since 1st class is only 1¢ more than 3rd class, I decided to travel that way and write a letter so it shouldn't be a waste even though I have nothing to say.

* The current transfiguration of my self-doubting old boss, colleague, protector and friend into the poetic celebrant of fly-fishing, Presbyterian virtue and—in the unfinished *Young Men and Fire* which, the day I write this, March 1, 1993, has been awarded the National Book Critics Prize for non-fiction—the heroic vocation of scholarship would have amazed, amused and fascinated him. (He'd spent years on an unfinished study of the wild young George Armstrong Custer's transfiguration into an American myth.) Low man on the Chicago English department's scholarly totem pole (he'd published but two or three tight-jawed articles), Norman battled booze, boredom and his sense of failure until, heroically, after his wonderful wife Jessie's death, he wrote his elegies for ruined young men. His sense of their fragility dominated his teaching as well as his books. Hundreds of students owe him much (including, perhaps, one of his co-winners today, our student Carol Brightman). Robert Redford's lyrical movie—though perhaps a bit too much river runs through it—surprised and even made me teary. Sitting among Chicago students, I understood much in Norman's feeling for them—and me.

It is a beautiful, clear fall day today and NY is at its best including the yowling Iranian students picketing MY hospital because of the Shah. I had a terrible fight with them last week—I was so enraged at their behavior. (I felt safe as there were 150 policemen standing next to me.) The next day Ralph told them their pictures of people killed by the Shah looked like the same ones killed by the Ayatollah and they accused him of being a member of the CIA (he was flattered). We do have a fun city!

Saw a great presentation last week—one-man Alec Woollcott show—really enjoyed it. No one is so literary and amusing anymore—now they'd probably have a square table [she's thinking of the Algonquin's Round Table]—or worse yet, junk food by a street stand. (Maybe that's the cause of it all—besides TV—no leisurely lunches.)

Off for my yogurt lunch.

Love, Ruth

I never looked forward to Ruth's letters, but it's clear, even from this, that she wrote well, was witty and observant. Wertheimer, the second-rate pianist in *The Loser,* spoke of his sister as "a page-turner." This is somewhat the way I thought of Ruth. Now—too late—I'm having second thoughts, some of Alcestis, who took her husband's place in hell because he was "necessary." She enchants Death, who allows her to return to earth. It's clear who was necessary. But unlike Alcestis, Ruth won't be back (except in this book).

Dream: Met mother and Ruth at a French restaurant on East Eighty-fifth. They were taking me to meet "my other sister," Ruth's twin, whom I saw and embraced. I asked why I hadn't known about her. Mother said she'd been in a hospital, cancerous, and had become bitter. I woke up, turned on WFMT, and heard two minutes of Rachmaninoff's First Symphony ("The Dream"!), of which—reported the announcer—César Cui had said, "If hell had a conservatory, and it commissioned a symphony for the seven plagues of Egypt, this would fit the bill."

At our Round Table I told the story about Uncle Gus's high-toned acquaintance, Otto Kahn. Walking past Temple Emanu-El with his hunchbacked friend, Marshall Wilder, he said, "I used to be a Jew." Wilder: "And I used to be a hunchback."

Ran into Mike Murrin, back from his summer in Mürren, a Swiss mountain village. He's teaching Bossuet's *oraison funebre* for Henriette, was amazed that I was reading it.

September 20. Ruth died a month ago tomorrow; it seems like a year.

Reading Irving's biography of Goering (who was named after his godfather, his mother's lover, Herman Eppenstein, a Jew). The Nazi's Third Kingdom (*Reich*) was supposed to last a thousand years but went through in a dozen years revolts, rebellions, assassinations, conquests and defeats that took Rome a millennium. Time-shrinkage, like the feeling that time passes more quickly each year. ("Every year's a smaller fraction of your life," is Hugh Kenner's explanation. Is the mathematics translated into *feeling?*)

The first poem I learned in school:

Solomon Grundy
Born on Monday
Christened on Tuesday
Married on Wednesday
Sick on Thursday
Worse on Friday
Died on Saturday
Buried on Sunday
And that is the end of Solomon Grundy.

Quickly, quickly. To learn such poems when we're six!

Woke at 3:30 after a dream of travel with Alane. She didn't want to go, so we returned to a California estate full of children, some of them mine—though not the ones I have. The word came that Ruth was in the house. I was surprised, I knew she was dead. She wasn't. She was lying in a shuttered room, the deathbed Ruth, but lively, not gaunt, just thin. Her legs were skinny and bare, and she gyrated in the bed. On her face was that erotic, playful look I saw in her dying days and which in the dream both alarmed and pleased me.

Saturday, September 21. A perfect autumn Saturday; the first season Ruth won't see.

September 23. Eyes still dilated, though I can read and write. Dr. Marianne Sandu, a Romanian emigrée with beautiful brown-green eyes, examined me first, then the young, long-haired Dr. Shaker, finally white-haired Dr. Norman Tepper, who's done "thousands" of these eye-straightening operations. No glaucoma or cataracts but there were two tiny rips in the operculum—cap—of the retina, so I saw the retinologist, Dr. Patel, who'll repair them with a laser.

September 24. Ralph called. He's been in Connecticut, seen Adele and Howard, Wilda and Marty, and Nancy O'Connell. He's played tennis, joined a film club and goes out once a week with Roger. They may go to Kate's for Thanksgiving. He's seeing lawyers and accountants about the estate, which he's having trouble disentangling. He has dreams of Ruth being lost.

Donald Lach's seventy-fourth birthday. Alma [Lach] ordered ice-cream sundaes for the Round Table. Next year the Press will publish the next twenty-two hundred pages of Donald's fifty-year project, *Asia in the Making of Europe*. (In a way it's even older: Donald got interested in Asia while he was in high school.)

September 26. Last night, heard, "Live from Lincoln Center," *The Marriage of Figaro*. I felt I *got* it. (Maybe it's the year I understand a few things.) It's no paean to revision; the countess's "forgiveness" is too brief. I think the opera throws farce over Mozart's social fury. (Mozart and DaPonte were also outsiders, DaPonte a converted Jew born Manny Rabbit-Warren (Conegliano) who left Italy and Vienna to teach Italian at Columbia.) The opera sets feeling against class. Almaviva (*Almamorte* would be closer to what he is) hates it that Figaro "enjoys what I can't have," the ability to feel. Music doesn't come just from music. "The best and truest of all friends are the poor," wrote Mozart. "The wealthy don't know what friendship means." You don't *hear* the whole opera if you don't hear this. Another brother to a sister four years older, Mozart was thought of as "childlike" (by Nannerl). (It took Ruth forty years to dislodge her early sense of me. It took me sixty to see her.)

Christopher called and talked for two hours. He'd been in the Catskills with his pals. He talked about wearing two pairs of pants and sweaters when he was twelve, mortified at his skinniness. "That only stopped when I ate my way from 167 to 210 on a Saturday Review expense account. A propos, I'm down to about two hundred." When I suggested he write about all these things, he said "It'd be as hard as writing a novel. I'm still fearful of making a mark." Gay had read him a birthday note I wrote her. "It was torn. I've gotten torn notes from you too." I didn't pursue this mystery.

October 1. I worked until midnight on the galleys of *Shares.* Three of the new stories and *Veni, Vidi . . . Wendt* looked okay, but I hated Wendt (the composer-narrator). Twenty years ago, I'd relished his anger and bitterness, thought they gave a special pulse to his sexual, paternal, marital and creative life. Now I think, "If this was me, no wonder Gay and the boys are on the couch."

Dr. Patel dilated me at 2:00, gave me a drop of topical anaesthetic at 2:15, turned on the water to cool the laser, lined up my eyes on the machine—a contact lens with triple mirrors over the eye—and blasted flashes into my eye. I sweated, sneezed, was sponged off, took a final blast and went home to a sleepless night, cursing Patel, convinced he'd overzapped me or missed the target. (A week later I thanked the courteous Patel for repairing the rips.)

Spoke to Andy. He's going with a woman who edits the *LaGrange Weekly,* Maryanne Costello. Saturdays, she takes a classics course here on campus. He'd had his Saturday basketball game. "The hook shot was sweet."

Oona O'Neill died, a year younger than Ruth. All those hard years taking care of the decaying Charlie. (He wouldn't let anyone else do it.) She carried around the picture of the father who wouldn't see her. I visited her in Vevey. The house reminded me of the Hermitage, another ex-poor boy's idea of class. Oona kept a journal; my guess is it's terrific. She was intelligent, literary and full of feeling which I'd guess didn't otherwise get expressed. I once mentioned to Claire how I'd loved Chaplin's return to Hollywood to get an Academy Award. His white hair and smile came out of the dark as the final close-up of *City Lights* faded. The audience cheered for minutes.

Richard Stern and Saul Bellow, Vermont

Claire laughed. "Oona said Charlie was saying, 'Fuck *you*, and fuck *you*, and fuck *you*.'"

Good talk with Saul, who's "dragging." His internist looked him over, there's nothing wrong, but it's hard to work. He did nothing today "but look at a few books." Of X, he said, "She practices friendship, she doesn't have any real feel for it. Like these ski-machines: she doesn't go out in real snow."

Nick is happier, has a new girl, has stopped smoking and biting his nails. Attributes it to the girl and his once-a-week therapy. "Everyone but you and Kate is in it." He said I was like the driver who hears cars crashing all around him and wonders why they let bad drivers on the road.

January 1, 1992. The first year Ruth will not see. In four days, she would have been sixty-eight.

I thought of Cal Lowell coming out of a Palmer House bathroom, his face half-mooned with lather, saying, "After you hit fifty, you think of death every day."

It hit me at sixty. After my hernia operation, I felt tremendous exhaustion; death seemed an easy next step. Only the thought of Alane being alone kept me back. Death hung around for days; then I walked, ate, grew stronger; life grew increasingly sweet.

Still, there was a gear shift. Most of my life I'd looked ahead. I'll do this, then that, go here, then there. The weekend, the summer, the next book. I didn't sense *an end*.

6 Coda

When does Ruth's story end?

January 1993. Ruth has—as I think it—"missed her second birthday." Last year, I called Ralph, and we told each other how strange it was that she wasn't *here*. This year I *meant* to but didn't call him.

Much has happened to Ralph since the funeral. He's been seeing a lot of Adele's sister, Norma. Norma, a widow for five years, lives in Syracuse, helping run a management institute for the university there. Her children are grown and gone. In September, she and Ralph went to England, then decided to live together. As I write, Ralph is en route to Syracuse to help her pack her stuff. This week, he emptied out a closet and found letters and clippings which he sent me, letters I'd sent my parents and Ruth these last forty-five years, pictures, reviews of my books. There were also pictures of Ruth with men whom she'd dated, none of whom I knew, one of whom Ralph had met. "This guy wouldn't speak to me. I guess Ruth jilted him." One picture was datelined Chicago, the year before they'd met. "Did you set her up with this guy?" I thought hard but couldn't remember the guy or, for that matter, Ruth's visit. Perhaps she'd come to see him and hadn't called me. A new wrinkle. How well did I know her? Ralph is also sending my mother's mink coat which Ruth had had remade. "It has the initials *RSL* on a pocket inside," said Ralph on the phone.

I told Alane, who said, "It'll be the best thing about the coat. Anyway where am I going to wear it?"

"Anywhere. Defiantly." I told her that the French equivalent of "radical chic" is *"le vison progrésiste,"* "progressive mink" (a phrase of Ionesco's).

A year ago, I thought that this version of Ruth's story came to an end the night of my sixty-fourth birthday, February 25, six months to the week after her death. (I'd thought of Cousin Felix (Mendelssohn) dying six months after his sister, Fanny.) The reason was I'd found blood in my stool. After I was cleaned out and x-rayed, the doctor said, "All clear."

The Saturday before my birthday, Willie, our odd-job man, asked if there was anything to do. I said, "There's a defective socket in the kitchen light fixture. Can you fix it?"

"Gimme a Phillips and a coat hanger."

"Sure?"

" 'Course I'm sure. Shut off the power."

I did. He poked at the wire with a meat fork.

"If you can't do it, forget it."

"Willya lemme alone?"

I went upstairs but, nervous, came back down. "How's it going?" A piece of coat-hanger neck was twisted around the light cones.

"It's fixed." He went down to turn on the power, and the lights went off. I called up to Alane. "Do you have lights up there?"

"No!"

Willie banged away at the circuit-breaker box. "You gotta flashlight?"

I went up to get one.

At the circuit board, all the slots but one read *On,* but the only things functioning were the furnace and the fridge.

"Dunno what went wrong."

I called electricians. Saturday, I got answering machines.

"Am I gonna git me somepin' outta this?"

"No."

"I don' have carfare." I handed him five dollars and, with unnatural calm, suggested he take off.

Alane spotted Gersh, a neighbor, and went out to ask him if he knew anything about electricity. He came back with a flashlight, looked things over and said, "Get an electrician."

"Nobody's around."

He said that our neighbor John Drazenovic's son was an electrician. "I saw him around today."

I called John, who said he was expecting his son in twenty minutes, he'd send him around. An hour or two later John Junior showed up, looked things over and said it was a big job. The power surge had backed up after Willie had shorted the light. "I'll get to it as soon as I can, probably Monday." He fixed up a small light in the study.

That night, exhausted, we skipped a farewell dinner with Philip, who, with Claire, had come in for the weekend. Sunday, rested and, in the light of day, peppier, I joined him after breakfast at the Bellows'. Janis and Saul hadn't seen my newly straightened eyes. Said Saul, "If I were an eighteen-year-old girl, I'd fall in love with you."

Monday, John Junior called to say that he'd had a big job, he'd try and get to us at 10:30 the next day. My birthday. We spent it waiting for him. I also waited for birthday calls (conscious there'd be one fewer call this year). We sat in my study. The waiting and my temper got worse. I called John Senior, who said somehow or other he'd get hold of his son.

At 6:30, Liza, Alex and Kate called and sang "Happy Birthday."

At 8:00, John Junior and his assistant—a cherubic-looking man recently arrived from Zagreb where his house had been bombed to smithereens—showed up with apologies. "I didn't have your phone number. I've canceled all other jobs tomorrow." He checked the dead smell of shorted tubes and burnt wires. "You should be all right overnight."

8:30. Andrew called and sang, "Will I still need you,/Will I still feed you,/When you're sixty-four?"

"You better."

At 10:00, Nick called. I told him our electrical saga and promised to show him my new eyes that summer.

10:15. Jeff called and sang "Happy Birthday."

Which accounted for everyone but Christopher (though I knew

that his *not calling* was more important for him than calling would have been for me).

10:30. Philip called, not for the birthday. "Your galleys arrived. Want me to read them?" (I'd told him how much I'd changed them.)

"You might as well."

"You sound gloomy."

"It's my birthday. Sixty-four, and I'm sitting in the dark." Then, suddenly thinking of Ruth, "But I guess I'm not the one in the dark."